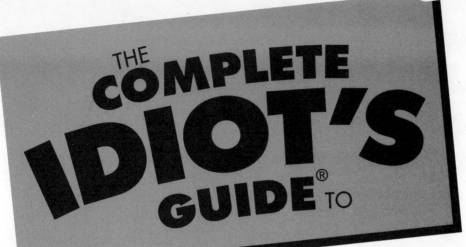

THE

COMPLETE IDIOT'S GUIDE® TO

Making Money with Mutual Funds for Canadians 🍁

Best copy Minul

THE COMPLETE IDIOT'S GUIDE® TO

Making Money with Mutual Funds for Canadians ✹

- ♦ **Simple steps** to build wealth, share by share
- ♦ **Quick and easy** strategies for choosing your investments
- ♦ **Valuable tips** to help you adjust your investment plan over time

Alan Lavine, Gail Liberman, & Stephen Nelson

An Alpha Books/Prentice Hall Canada Copublication

Prentice Hall Canada Inc., Scarborough, Ontario

Canadian Cataloguing in Publication Data

Lavine, Alan
    The complete idiot's guide to making money with mutual funds for Canadians

Includes index.
ISNB 0-13-082536-0

1. Mutual Funds — Canada. I. Liberman, Gail, 1951–   . II. Nelson, Stephen, 1968–   . III. Title.

HG4530.L36 1998   332.63'27   C98-932066-9

 © 1998 Prentice-Hall Canada Inc., Ontario
A Division of Simon & Schuster/A Viacom Company

Prentice-Hall, Inc., Upper Saddle River, New Jersey
Prentice-Hall International (UK) Limited, London
Prentice-Hall of Australia, Pty. Limited, Sydney
Prentice-Hall Hispanoamericana, S.A., Mexico City
Prentice-Hall of India Private Limited, New Delhi
Prentice-Hall of Japan, Inc., Tokyo
Simon & Schuster Southeast Asia Private Limited, Singapore
Editora Prentice-Hall do Brasil, Ltda., Rio de Janeiro

ISBN 0-13-082536-0

Director, Trade Group: Robert Harris
Copy Editor: Karen Rolfe
Assistant Editor: Joan Whitman
Production Editor: Lu Cormier
Production Coordinator: Shannon Potts
Art Direction: Mary Opper
Cover Design: Kyle Gell
Cover Photograph: Ralph Mercer, Tony Stone Images
Page Layout: Gail Ferreira Ng-A-Kien

1 2 3 4 5   RRD   02 01 00 99 98

Printed and bound in the United States of America

This publication contains the opinions and ideas of its authors and is designed to provide useful advice in regard to the subject matter covered. The authors and publisher are not engaged in rendering legal, accounting, or other professional services in this publication. This publication is not intended to provide a basis for action in particular circumstances without consideration by a competent professional. The authors and publisher expressly disclaim any responsibility for any liability, loss, or risk, personal or otherwise, which is incurred as a consequence, directly or indirectly, of the use and application of any of the contents of this book.

Visit the Prentice Hall Canada Web site! Send us your comments, browse our catalogues, and more.
www.phcanada.com

*I would like to dedicate this book to
Bill Nelson and Dave Nelson.*

Contents At A Glance

Contents

Part 1: Mutual Funds: What Are They? What Are They Not? Are They For You? **1**

1 The Ten Commandments of Mutual Fund Investing **3**

2 Mutual Funds: To Own or Not to Own? **9**

3 Investing: Your Options, Your Risks, Your Rewards **17**

Acknowledgements

I would like to thank my assistant Janet Yu who, as with the first book, put a great deal of time and hard work into this project.

I would also like to thank Greg Nott, who took time out of his busy daily schedule to answer all our questions.

Last, but not least, I would like to acknowledge the following people:

Kathryn Nelson, Debbie Nelson, Kathy Nelson, Denise Guerriere, Theresa Foran, Julie Wilson, Seána Campbell-Wood, Kelsey Ham, Daphne Dias, Candace Hummel, Patty Dilworth, Cathy Taylor Veres, Carole Pelan, and Wendy Gardner.

About the Author

Stephen Nelson is a graduate of the Economics program at the University of Western Ontario, and currently works as a Senior Investment Advisor at TD Evergreen, TD Bank's full-service brokerage firm. His clients include individuals, institutions, and non-profit organizations. Stephen has been servicing his clients for over nine years and has built a wealth of knowledge in fixed income and equity markets.

He is also the author of the bestseller *The Complete Idiot's Guide to Making Money on the Stock Market.*

Stephen can be reached at (416) 982–8670, or by e-mail at **nelsos3@tdbank.ca**.

Foreword

In virtually all the industrialized nations, governments have delivered the message loud and clear: We will take responsibility for our fiscal housekeeping. Your personal financial future is up to you.

In your hands right now is an excellent first step to take control of your future. The financial markets can be intimidating for new investors. Using plain language and a logical format, this book sets out important signposts, demystifies financial jargon, and attempts to help you find the shortest, smoothest route to investing success.

As you gain confidence in your understanding of mutual funds, the next essential step is to join forces with a professional financial advisor who can help formulate and carry out a workable financial plan for your circumstances. I cannot stress enough the importance of taking full advantage of the special skills and knowledge accumulated by experienced investment industry professionals.

Responsibility and privilege—like risk and reward—are flip sides of the same coin. It is always satisfying for us in the investment industry to watch an investor's appetite for self-direction increase as the benefits become apparent. The paths to financial security requires patience and determination, but the reward is an independence that makes the journey well worth the effort.

David R. McBain
Senior Vice-President
C.I. Mutual Funds

Introduction

You've heard about mutual funds. Maybe you've read about them. Or you might know someone who has invested in them. Getting started is easier said than done, however. Invest your hard-earned savings based on what your friends, neighbours, or co-workers say is hot, and you're sure to get stung. In fact, you probably have friends who already are crying in their beer over their ill-fated investment decisions.

As a Senior Investment Advisor, I understand your need to avoid these scenarios. I advise clients day in and day out, helping them reach their financial goals. Mutual fund investing provides a means to meeting those goals. With the over 1800 mutual funds available in Canada today, there are a wide variety of options available. But, before you begin investing, we have to cover the basics— which is just what this book sets out to do.

With *The Complete Idiot's Guide to Making Money with Mutual Funds*, you easily can locate all the information you need— both before and long after you take your first venture into mutual funds. And once I help you determine whether mutual fund investing is right for you, I'll present you with quick and uncomplicated ways of managing your stash and making your hard-earned dollars work for you.

I've taken all the jargon out of investing and spelled things out in plain English so that learning to invest is as easy as learning to ride a bike. Consider this book my gift to you so that you and your family can reap the most possible out of your money. It's just a matter of doing a little homework, learning exactly how these things work, and making your own decisions based only on sound financial planning and a little research.

This book is a starting point. It will help you

> ➤ Learn how mutual funds work and what they invest in

> ➤ Understand the stock and bond markets

> ➤ Find the mutual fund investment that's best for you

> ➤ Avoid losses

> ➤ Build your wealth long term

> ➤ Invest for your child's post-secondary education

> ➤ Invest for retirement

> ➤ Manage your investments

> ➤ Save on taxes.

How to Use This Book

The Complete Idiot's Guide to Making Money with Mutual Funds zeros in on all the important things you need to know to invest in mutual funds. Start now. Read this book and learn the keys to a happy and healthy financial future. The important details about mutual funds are covered in five parts.

Part 1, "Mutual Funds: What Are They? What Are They Not? Are They for You?" explains how mutual funds work. This section nails down the dos and don'ts of mutual fund investments and shows you how to develop a savings plan. You'll learn all about stocks and bonds, as well as the benefits and drawbacks of mutual fund investing. You'll also get a rundown of the different types of mutual funds and learn how to tell whether a fund is a winner or loser.

Part 2, "Getting Started," helps you discover exactly what types of investing you can handle without hitting the antacid bottle. Then you'll learn how to locate funds that are right for you. You'll also learn where to get mutual funds and how much you'll pay for them. You'll learn how to track down the best fund deals. You'll also learn about the resources available to help you pick your mutual funds.

Part 3, "Zoning In on the Picks," gets to the nitty-gritty. You'll learn how money market funds work . You'll learn about the different types of bond funds available to investors and the risks they carry. Chapter 14, on stock funds, looks at all the types of stock funds—from aggressive, small company, growth, and growth and income to international—and what they invest in. You'll also learn about stock funds for special situations.

Part 4, "The One-Hour-a-Year Investment Plans," gives you time-saving tools to manage your money like a pro. This section reviews several easy-to-use investment strategies to build your wealth. You'll learn how to invest regularly so that you automatically keep buying fund units at low prices. You'll also learn a couple of easy ways to buy low and sell high—just in case you prefer to take your profits and run. You'll learn how to slice your mutual fund investment pie to get the best returns with the least risk. You'll also find a really low-risk way to invest your retirement savings in mutual funds and beat the performance of the old bank account.

Part 5, "Financial Planning" reviews important issues you need to know when you invest in mutual funds. Unfortunately, you have to pay Revenue Canada on your mutual fund profits. In this part, you'll learn the most painless ways to do it. Chapter 19, on saving for important life goals, shows how to determine the amount of money you'll need for your child's post-secondary education and your retirement.

Extras

We built a launch pad for you to get started with mutual funds. To make it as simple as turning your car's ignition switch, *The Complete Idiot's Guide to Making Money with Mutual Funds* is chock full of tips to ensure that you have a successful trip into the world of mutual funds. Look for these elements in the book to point you in the right direction:

Sidelines

This is your coach sitting on the sidelines telling you how to navigate through the investment maze. You learn extra little details to make even better investment decisions.

Technobabble

Want to talk the same language as the investment pros? No problem. It's all highlighted for you as a quick reference in these little boxes.

Look Out!

Watch these potholes on the road to successful mutual fund investing! These tips tell you what to avoid so you can save money in the long run.

Hot Tip

Hot tips help you invest. We cut through the red tape and tell you straight out the wisest moves. You'll learn quickly the best route to take on your mutual fund journey.

The Complete Idiot's Guide to Making Money with Mutual Funds for Canadians

Part 1
Mutual Funds: What Are They? What Are They Not? Are They For You?

Once you read this part of the book, you'll be richer than you are. After all, you've got to have money before you can invest in mutual funds, right?

In this part, you discover ways to come up with money you didn't know you had. You learn what's involved in becoming an investor.

You also learn about the advantages and disadvantages of mutual funds in particular. There are a tremendous variety of mutual funds to choose from. When you know what options are out there, you can zero in on what is right for you.

Chapter 1

The Ten Commandments of Mutual Fund Investing

> ## In This Chapter
>
> ➤ How mutual funds work
>
> ➤ Who runs the funds?
>
> ➤ How mutual funds are regulated
>
> ➤ Ten rules to live by

Let's face it. You had good reason to pick up this book. After all, everybody's talking about mutual funds these days.

If you're like most of us, you have the bulk of your money in bank savings accounts because you're afraid you'll make the wrong move. Your biggest investment probably is your home. Some of you might have an interest in company pension plans. Aside from that, and maybe some money tucked away each paycheque in an RRSP, investing is a mystery.

Get ready! A whole new world of investing is about to unfold before your eyes. Fear no more. Mutual funds, once you know the ropes, can be your ticket to a whole variety of money-making opportunities. This chapter introduces you to mutual fund investing.

Welcome to the World of Investing

When you were younger, you had a piggy bank. When you filled it up, you took the next big step. You carted it to the bank and opened a savings account. You knew your savings account was safe. You couldn't lose money. Every once in a while, assuming you left your money in there, you'd notice it was growing in value.

With your savings account, you couldn't lose any money because it was federally insured. You paid dearly for this sense of security, though. About the most you can earn in a savings account these days is two percent.

Investing is the next big step on the ladder to financial growth for those who want to make more.

When you enter the world of investing, you're giving yourself a promotion. You're taking a more active role in building your wealth and stand to make more as a result. By putting your money in a mutual fund, however, you're also giving up some of the safety and security of your piggy bank and savings account. If you learn what makes mutual funds tick, you can make educated investment decisions that can help your nest egg grow that much more.

What Is a Mutual Fund and How Does It Work?

Think of a mutual fund as an investment company that pools the money of people just like you for one common reason—to make more. Not all pots of money, though, are alike. Each mutual fund has its own strategy and investment objective for making money. It's up to you to select the right mutual fund for you based on your own needs.

There are two types of mutual funds. The most common, which this book primarily talks about, is *open-end* funds. In essence, they are open—money flows directly into the fund when investors buy and goes directly out when they sell. The other type is *closed-end* funds, which, although frequently grouped with mutual funds, are not techically mutual funds. You'll learn about them in Chapter 15.

With a mutual fund, the big pool of money we talked about previously is managed by a company, which is frequently the organization that started the fund. This management company or the mutual fund company either serves as or hires the fund's portfolio manager. The portfolio manager and his or her research staff select investments for the mutual fund.

Mutual funds are subject to strict regulation. The mutual fund company is required to send you a prospectus when you invest in one of their funds for the first time. You can also request a prospectus before you invest. The *prospectus* is an important document that spells out the investment objectives of the fund, risks, fees, and other important information. In Chapter 9 you'll learn more about what's in a prospectus and what you should look for.

Generally, mutual funds continuously offer new units to the public. When you sell units in a fund, you receive proceeds based on its unit's price or *net asset value* (less any sales charges, if applicable). The net asset value is obtained when the fund figures the value of its investments, less liabilities, divided by the number of units outstanding at the end of the day.

The Cast of a Mutual Fund

Like any company, the mutual fund management company is an organization with a number of people who run the show. You want to understand their responsibilities because you've entrusted them with your hard-earned cash.

The mutual fund management company typically hires the portfolio manager to manage your mutual fund. They also may make arrangements to have the fund sold through a brokerage firm.

Let's review the cast of characters who make a mutual fund work.

The Portfolio Manager

The portfolio manager and his or her team make the investment decisions. You've probably seen some portfolio managers on TV, spotted their quotes in magazines, or read some of their books. This person selects, buys, and sells the investments based on the fund's investment objective. The portfolio manager is usually paid a salary as well as a bonus based on the assets of the mutual fund as well as a bonus based on the performance of the fund.

The Unitholder

Mutual fund investors are known as unitholders. When you invest in a mutual fund, you actually buy a unit or portion of a mutual fund. Each unit has a price tag. If a fund sells for $10 a unit and you invest $1000, you're the proud owner of 100 units of the fund!

Technobabble

A *portfolio manager* is the professional who actually manages the fund. The *investment objective* describes what your mutual fund hopes to accomplish. *Assets* represent any investment that the mutual fund holds, including stocks, bonds, and cash reserves. A mutual fund *unit* is a unit of ownership in the fund. A mutual fund investor who owns units is called a *unitholder*.

Custodians and Transfer Agents

As you can imagine, the millions of mutual fund transactions executed each year require a gargantuan behind-the-scenes record-keeping effort. The securities a mutual fund invests in are kept under lock and key by an appointed *custodian*, usually a bank. The custodian may respond only to instructions from fund officers responsible for dealing with the custodian. The custodian safeguards the fund's assets, makes payments for the fund's securities, and receives payments when securities are sold.

5

Fund *transfer agents* maintain unitholder account records, including purchases, sales, and account balances. They also authorize the payments made by the custodian, prepare and mail account statements, maintain a customer service department to respond to account inquiries, and provide federal income tax information, unitholder notices, and confirmation statements.

Mutual Funds Make It Easy to Invest

Boy, there are a lot of ingredients that go into the making of a mutual fund. The end result, however, is that mutual funds provide one of the simplest ways to invest—especially if you count yourself among us working stiffs, and lack time and training to manage money like the Bay Street big boys.

The major difference between investing in a mutual fund and investing in an individual stock or bond is that with a mutual fund, instead of buying just one stock or bond, you really buy a portion of a variety of investments. Exactly how much money you make or lose in your mutual fund can change daily, as you'll learn in later chapters. It all depends on how many units you own and how well your mix of investments performs. As Chapter 3 explains, owning a lot of different investments helps to protect you against losing money. If one investment in your mutual fund does poorly, you have a number of others to cushion the blow.

Here They Are: The 10 Commandments

Are you still paying attention? Good. Let's get ready to proceed. However, we don't want you to invest one penny in a mutual fund until you read and thoroughly digest these 10 critical rules of mutual fund investing:

1. **Always understand exactly what you're investing in.** You can lose a bundle if you pick the wrong kind of mutual fund. Carefully read the prospectus and other literature that mutual fund companies provide on their funds.

2. **Don't rush out and buy the first mutual fund that looks good.** You first have to identify your investment goals, determine how much you need from your investment (see Chapter 2), and figure out how much you're willing to risk losing (see Chapter 6).

3. **Don't try to make quick profits.**
Always try to invest for the long term.
If your time horizon allows it, you
should plan to hold your mutual
funds a minimum of five to ten years.

4. **Mix up your investments.** You can
cut your chances of losing money
by putting your money in different
types of investments. Chapter 7 shows
you how.

5. **Invest regularly with each paycheque—before you have a
chance to spend all your money.**
Mutual funds have automatic investment programs, which means money
is electronically taken out of your bank
account and invested in the fund.

6. **Do your homework.** Once you determined how much money you need
and by when—as well as how much
you can afford to lose—research the best investments to meet your goals.

> **Sidelines**
>
> You can buy mutual funds directly
> from your full-service broker,
> discount broker, or financial
> planner licensed to sell them, to
> name a few. Full-service brokers
> offer advice and hand holding if
> required. For the most part,
> discount brokers don't offer you
> any advice/services beyond the
> execution of the mutual fund buy
> or sell order. Chapter 7 explains
> your options in more detail.

7. **Seek professional advice.** There are an infinite number of investment
advisors and mutual fund salespeople who can answer your questions. Ask
your friends and family for references.

8. **Make sure your mutual fund investment earns enough so that
your nest egg at least keeps pace with rising prices.** Chapter 5 discusses this further.

9. **Know when to sell your mutual funds.** Chapter 16 explains ways to
evaluate how a fund is doing. You'll learn when to get rid of a mutual fund
that's a lemon.

10. **Invest to beat the tax man.** Take advantage of Registered Retirement
Savings Plans (RRSPs) and other tax shelters. Chapter 19 discusses how you
can make tax-deductible contributions and watch your money grow tax-free
until you retire.

The Least You Need to Know

➤ With a mutual fund, investors pool their money with one common goal—to
make more.

➤ A mutual fund's investment decisions are made by the portfolio manager, who has been hired by the mutual fund company.

➤ When you invest in a mutual fund, you own unit(s) of the fund.

➤ Try to invest for the long term.

that is the question...

Chapter 2

Mutual Funds: To Own or Not to Own?

In This Chapter

➤ Zeroing in on your goals

➤ Starting a savings plan

➤ Scrounging up enough money to invest

Do you need extra cash in time for your next rent payment? Are you a teenager looking to start saving for university? Or are you a retiree who wants to increase your very limited income over the next five years?

Regardless of who you are, it never hurts to raise a little extra cash for the cause—and nobody wants to lose money in the markets, right?

We hear ya on both counts. In this chapter, you learn how to figure out how much you'll need and by when. As Thomas A. Edison would testify if he were here today, a plan is Step One toward getting where you want to go. That's what this chapter is all about.

Is Father Time on Your Side?

Your age has a lot to do with how you save. Unless you're a Rockefeller, 20- and 30-year-olds typically don't have as much money to invest as people who have been working for 20 years.

Nevertheless, younger investors do have an important advantage when it comes to investing. They have more time for their money to grow. Big-ticket events such as retirement and children's educations are farther away, so it's all right for young people to put a little less away on a regular basis. Plus, they have all those years to watch their money grow.

If you're in your 40s and just getting into mutual funds, you have a shorter period to save for retirement, so you might need to save more. Get into your 60s, and it may be more important to keep what you already have to meet your everyday living expenses.

How does all this relate to mutual funds?

Probably the most critical factor in figuring out how or whether to invest in mutual funds is determining when you need your money. It also influences which mutual funds you choose. You will learn in the following chapters the advantages of investing in mutual funds and what funds are right for your situation. However, mutual fund investing should be a long-term affair. History has shown repeatedly that over the long term—say, five to ten years—most mutual funds perform substantially better than bank savings accounts or GICs. History also has proven that the longer you have to invest in a mutual fund, the slimmer your chance of losing money. That's why it's important to get a fix on your investment goals and how long you have to invest.

Setting Your Goals

If you're like most Canadian families, this part of our exercise will astound you. When you see on paper the money you're going to need throughout your life, there's a good chance you'll want to hop right on a space shuttle and move to another planet!

Don't get discouraged. Fortunately, mutual funds and other types of investments are here to help you achieve your goals. The sooner you start planning, the better off you'll be. As astounded as you are at the staggering costs most people encounter in their lifetimes, you'll be just as surprised when you see how quickly your money can grow.

Technobabble

Your *goals* are all your future desires. A *spending plan* is a strategy to help cut wasteful spending so you can invest.

Huh? Why Do I Need to Invest?

First, find a comfortable chair. Then sit down with a pad and pencil and jot down all the reasons you'll need more money in the future. Rank those goals from most to least important.

The next step is to figure how much each will cost. The Investment Goals Worksheet in this chapter will help.

To organize your thoughts, first zero in on every money worry you have. Cars, unfortunately, need to be repaired. Teeth need to be fixed. No doubt, you've got out-of-town guests who need to be taken out to dinner. What about emergency trips or urgent household repairs?

Next, list your short-term goals. Most people buy a car about every five years. That's going to cost you some big bucks. The way new car prices are rising, in a few years the average new car will cost us $20,000 to $25,000. Ah, what if you've been dreaming about buying a house in five or six years? You may need $20,000 to $25,000 for a down payment. You'll also need money—$10,000 plus—to furnish it.

Once you cover emergencies and the stuff you need, it's time to focus on longer-term needs. If you're going to send a child who is now an infant to university in some 18 years, expect to pay a whopping $30,000 to $40,000 a year by the time Junior's ready. Looking to retire? If you're making $35,000 annually now, you need about $500,000 earning seven percent interest annually to make the same amount, discounting the impact of inflation. Chapters 12, 13, and 14 of this book will help you find the right mutual funds to help you meet long-term needs.

Next, think about those little luxuries. Sure, you don't *have* to have it, but wouldn't it be nice to have a yacht and a winter home in Florida?

Now that you've got your financial necessities and desires down on paper and ranked in order of importance, attach a price tag to each. Figure out how much each is likely to cost.

Finally, look at the time frame you have to invest for each of your goals. For example, if you've just had a baby, you have 18 years before your child will be ready for university. That's 18 years you have to come up with the cash. If you're driving an old clunker, you may have to shell out $20,000 for a new car a year from now. That's not much time at all!

Once you have your financial plan mapped out, you can start socking away your cash. You can take advantage of mutual funds to invest in a tax-advantaged savings plan for your child such as a Registered Education Savings Plan or RESP (discussed further in Chapter 19).

If you've never saved much before, it's time to start. You should keep a small cash reserve on hand to meet any emergencies. This money needs to be in a secure place where you can access it right away e.g., a money market mutual fund. You don't want to be forced to take losses on your investments because you need quick cash. In Chapter 11, you'll learn all about money market mutual funds. These are the least risky mutual fund investments. Even better—you'll earn a higher return than with a regular savings or chequing account.

Hot Tip

Don't put off making a financial plan until tomorrow! Try to cut some of those frivolous expenses so you can meet your objectives.

Table 2.1 Investment Goals Worksheet

Goal	Amount You Need	When You Need It
Cash reserves		
Retirement		
Child's post-secondary education		
Second home down payment		
Travel		
Estate		
Other		

Create a worksheet like this to help set your investment goals.

If you've already invested in mutual funds, you might be ready to try some new investments. In Chapter 6, you'll also learn to determine your *risk tolerance*, which is how much money you can stomach losing in any given year. Then, you'll be able to put both pieces of information together to make the right kinds of mutual fund investments.

Starting a Savings Plan

You want to invest in mutual funds to meet your goals. "But I have no money," you balk. Regardless of whether you have money to invest, it always pays to squeeze as much as you possibly can out of your budget for investing.

This needn't be as painful as it sounds. We're willing to bet you have more cash than you think sitting right under your nose.

To figure out exactly where you stand, first list and then add up your monthly income from your paycheque, savings, and other sources. Then, get your chequebook register and list all your monthly expenses. The worksheet below will help you. Then, subtract your expenses from your income to determine the amount of cash you should have available to invest monthly.

Table 2.2 Finding Money to Invest

Finding Money to Invest

Monthly Income

Paycheck (after taxes) _____

Other _____

Total Income: _____

Monthly Spending

Rent or mortgage _____

Utilities _____

Groceries and Dining Out _____

Clothing _____

Entertainment _____

Vacations _____

Car payments _____

Car repairs _____

Gas _____

Car insurance _____

Life insurance _____

Disability insurance _____

Child care _____

Child support or alimony _____

Gifts _____

Educational expenses _____

Pet expenses _____

Newspapers and magazines _____

Hobbies _____

Miscellaneous expenses _____

Credit cards and loans _____

Total Expenses: _____

**Monthly Cash
(Income - Expenses)** _____

Use this worksheet to get a better handle on the cash you might have available for investing and to see whether there are any areas where you might be spending too much.

Things to Attack Right Away

Whether the money you have left for investing is a large sum or a big fat zero, it's time to set up a spending (and savings) plan for next year—including, without fail, money to invest!

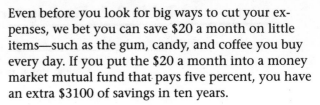

Even before you look for big ways to cut your expenses, we bet you can save $20 a month on little items—such as the gum, candy, and coffee you buy every day. If you put the $20 a month into a money market mutual fund that pays five percent, you have an extra $3100 of savings in ten years.

Now, examine each item in your expenses line by line to find any areas you might cut to free even more money.

Credit card debts are a good place to start. You may pay more than 20 plus percent interest on your credit card bills. If you first pay those off, you'll get a better return than on many mutual funds.

Vacations are another expense worth reviewing. Rather than going to Aruba, maybe you can find a nice resort close to home. You still can have a good time and save a bundle.

Sidelines

The biggest expense you can cut right now is debt. As you accumulate more debt, the harder it will be to dig yourself out. Start by cutting up those credit cards. You might want to consult your banker to see if you can consolidate all your loans into one and pay a reduced rate of interest.

Manage Your Money Like a Pro

You'd be surprised what a little savvy cash management can do for your long-term financial picture. Why not take some tips from professional money managers, whose job it is to use efficient cash-management tactics to make their money work for them?

Here are a few ways to manage your cash like a pro. By following these guidelines, you can free as much as $150 a year for investing. That annual investment, earning a rate of 5 percent, can grow over 20 years to an extra $4,960 for retirement—not a bad reward for no lifestyle cutbacks.

Hot Tip

Need some help getting started? Pick up the *Canadian Guide to Personal Financial Management* by Deloitte & Touche, published by Prentice Hall.

The key to cash management is to invest your money right away and pay your bills at the end of the month. You may already have an interest-bearing chequing account, but you also can take advantage of higher interest rates and invest in a money market fund (discussed in Chapters 4 and 11 of this book). Then, follow this plan:

➤ Deposit all your cheques as soon as you receive them; then you will earn interest right away.

➤ Avoid all bank fees. When you withdraw money from ATM machines other than your own bank's machines, for example, you pay as much as $2.00 on every transaction.

➤ Make use of your employer's payroll direct-deposit program. The money is electronically credited to your interest-bearing chequing account and earns interest immediately. Some institutions waive chequing fees if you direct-deposit your paycheque.

➤ Along the same lines, if you automatically have money taken out of your interest-bearing chequing account to pay insurance or mortgage bills, do it at the end of the month. That way your money earns interest for a full month before you pay those bills.

➤ Charge smart. As long as you have no outstanding balance on your Visa™ or MasterCard™, for example, you have a 25-day grace period each month before the bill is due. Try to make your purchases at the very beginning of the billing cycle (just after the monthly closing date). Then you'll have 25 days before the credit card company bills you, plus 10 days or more before you have to pay the bill.

The Least You Need to Know

➤ Always know how much you'll need and by when.

➤ Monitor your monthly income and expenses.

➤ Adjust the way you spend to free extra cash for investing.

Chapter 3

Investing:
Your Options,
Your Risks,
Your Rewards

In This Chapter

➤ What's inside mutual funds?

➤ What is a stock?

➤ What is a bond?

➤ What is a money market investment?

Are you getting ready to join the club? Canadians are continuing to invest in mutual funds at a strong pace. According to the Investment Funds Institute of Canada, as of April 1998, over $329 billion was invested in mutual funds in Canada. So, what exactly are Canadians putting their money into? Before you purchase any fund, you should understand the different types of mutual funds available to you.

Mutual funds come in a variety of models. You wouldn't buy that new car without first checking the tires and looking under the hood.

This chapter pops open the hood on mutual fund investments. It explains how mutual funds invest and the advantages mutual funds have to offer.

Stocks Versus Bonds Versus Cash

Congrats! In Chapter 2 you probably came up with money you didn't even know you had. Before you get excited and plunk down all the cash you just worked so hard to dig up, you need to know about all the critters that can hang out in a mutual fund.

Earlier, we mentioned stocks, bonds, or cash investments that you normally buy directly from a stockbroker. Stockbrokers have one word for all this stuff—*securities*.

A mutual fund may invest in one type of security or a mix of different kinds of securities. A mutual fund's value may rise or fall quite rapidly—or slowly—depending on the types of securities investments it makes. The exception is money market mutual funds, which are designed in most cases, to maintain a constant share value, usually $10 per share.

The following sections offer a rundown of the kinds of securities you're apt to find in a mutual fund and how each affects how much money you may make from your mutual fund investment.

Stocks

Stocks provide a way for a company to raise money. The company sells stock shares in exchange for money to use to grow the business—by buying new equipment or performing research and development, for example. If you or your mutual fund own shares of a company's stock, you're a big shot. Not only are you part owner of that company, but you may get to share in its earnings, which may be distributed to shareholders in the form of *dividends*. If the mutual fund owns shares of a particular dividend-paying stock, it pays these dividends to you, based on the number of mutual fund units you own.

If the company profits, it's good news. The share price of the stock can increase, which, in turn, hikes the value of its shares. The company's board of directors may vote to increase dividends they pay shareholders.

Unfortunately, the opposite also can happen. If the company does poorly, the value of the stock may decline, and dividends may be cut or eliminated entirely.

> **Techobabble**
>
> There are two major types of stocks—*common* and *preferred*. If you own preferred stock, you receive the dividends before common stockholders. You also get preferred treatment over common stockholders when it comes to getting your investment back if the company goes under. Preferred stocks tend to pay slightly higher dividends than common stock, but the share price usually doesn't rise as much. Most individual stockholders and mutual funds own <u>common stock</u>.

Stocks probably are one of the riskiest investments for individuals and mutual funds. Not only might the fund earn a ton of money in stocks before you have a chance to blink, but also the fund can lose just as much just as quickly.

Bonds

A *bond* is an IOU issued by a company or a city, province, or federal government or its agencies. When you buy a bond, you're the lender. In exchange for a loan, the borrower or *issuer* promises to repay the money on a specific date, known as the *maturity date*. If you or your mutual fund own a bond, you, as lender, receive fixed periodic interest payments. Bonds require a minimum investment of at least $1000, which is also know as the *face value* or principal. After you buy your bond, you or your mutual fund can hold it to maturity and get the principal back, or you can sell it before maturity.

Bonds can be tricky little devils to understand. There are three ways that describe how much interest income you will receive from a bond. It's important to understand the distinctions.

The *coupon* rate, which we will call the stated interest rate, tells you the interest payment in dollars that you will receive from the bond as a percentage of the bond's face value. Suppose for example, you buy a newly issued bond for $1000 and it has a coupon rate of 9 percent. That means you receive a total of $90 in interest income from the bond for the year. Year in and year out you will collect $90 from the bond until it matures. Then you get your $1000 back.

Bonds have two yields: the *current yield* is based on the current market price of the bond rather than the face value. If a bond with a face value of $1000 declines in value to $900, it still earns $90 a year in interest income, based on the bond's stated interest rate. As a result, the current yield of the bond is $90 divided by $900, or 10 percent.

You also have to consider a bond's *yield to maturity*. Bonds typically pay semi-annual interest over a specific time period. The interest compounds twice a year as long as you own the bond until it matures. The yield to maturity of a bond includes not only this semi-annual compounding of interest, but also the capital gain, or profit or loss, on the security itself.

How Bonds Are Classified

Federal government bonds are backed by the full faith and credit of the Canadian government. Corporate bonds are not. Once you go beyond the federal government, you have to make sure you invest in financially strong companies, provinces, or cities. That's why it's important to look at bond credit ratings.

Companies such as the Dominion Bond Rating Service (DBRS) and the Canadian Bond Rating Service (CBRS) rate the financial strength of bond issuers, based on the ability of companies or governments to repay principal and interest on time. The highest-quality bonds are rated AAA. Bonds rated below single A stand a greater chance of failing to repay their debts during tough economic times. Unless you're a seasoned investor, you might want to stay clear of investing in bonds with lower ratings.

Other Bond Risks

When you buy bonds or invest in bond funds, you not only have to look at the issuers' financial strengths, but you also must deal with changing bond prices.

Chapters 12 and 13 discuss the risks and ratings of bonds in more detail, but it is important to note that you can get into trouble even with the highest-quality bonds if you're not careful. Interest rates and bond prices move in opposite directions, so it's not always a time for rejoicing if interest rates head up. It means that your bonds are losing value if their coupon rates (stated interest rates) are less than the going rates.

Put yourself in a bond-buyer's shoes. If you could buy a newly issued bond paying a stated interest rate of 10 percent by investing $1000, you certainly wouldn't offer Joe Biddle the same $1000 for his bond paying a stated rate of 9 percent, would you? Unless you can buy the bond for less money, it's simply not worth putting up your hard-earned cash for a lower yield.

That's exactly how the big bond traders think. Moreover, the longer the term (time to maturity) of the bond, the riskier it appears to the bond investor and the less it is valued. Why? The longer the term, the greater the period an investor has to worry about the threat of rising interest rates.

If interest rates rise one percent, a two-year Government of Canada Bond loses nearly two percent in value. By contrast, a 30-year Government of Canada Bond loses about 12 percent in value. Chapter 13 shows you exactly how much rate shifts can affect bond prices.

If you need to sell your bond before maturity you may suffer a loss. However, like most people, if you hold your bond till maturity, you will continue to receive interest payments until maturity when you get back your principal, or your original investment. (This, of course applies so long as the issuer does not default on payment.)

Believe it or not, bond investors also might get their principal back faster than they'd like. That's because issuers may have the right to call their bonds or return the bondholder's principal. Bonds get called when interest rates fall. The issuer then sells lower-yielding bonds and reduces its interest payments.

Kinds of Bonds a Fund May Own

You typically can find the following variety of bonds in your mutual fund if it invests in bonds:

➤ Government of Canada Bonds issued by the federal government of Canada.

➤ Provincial bonds issued by provinces in Canada.

➤ Municipal bonds issued by individual municipalities in Canada.

➤ Corporate bonds issued by companies.

➤ International bonds issued by foreign corporations or governments.

Money Market Investments

Money market investments are short-term loans (usually less than a year) to banks, governments, or companies. Some of the more common money market instruments include Treasury Bills (T-bills), Bankers' Acceptances (BAs), and Commercial Paper (CP). T-bills are offered and backed by the Canadian government. BAs are bank-guaranteed notes that offer excellent yields and good security. Commercial Paper is issued by corporations and offers the best short-term yields, but is not guaranteed.

The Risk of Going It Alone

The good news is that any of the securities just discussed has the potential to do better (and in some cases much better!) than your faithful savings account.

The bad news, as we warned you earlier, is that the value of bonds can fluctuate between the time of purchase and the maturity date. So, if you have to sell your bond prior to maturity—beware!

You've probably heard the horror stories yourself. Joe Biddle's neighbour has a hot stock tip on a company that makes 3D video games. "Buy the stock," the neighbour whispers. "Double your money in a couple of days. Buy now and sell when everybody gets wind of this deal."

Aha! Joe empties his bank account and buys 500 shares at $10 a share for a total investment of $5000. The next day he opens the newspaper. "Video Games Cause Creepy Slime Disease," the headline blares. Wham! The next day, everyone sells. The stock's price plunges to $5 a share. Worried that it soon could drop to zero, he also sells. Joe's loss: $2500 or half of his investment.

A similar situation could happen with a bond if Joe happens to invest in a weak company (say, with a BB rating) that falls on tough times. Suppose Joe, based on his neighbour's advice, invests $5000 in a new bond issued by the same 3D video game company. Investors get wind of the fact that the company may have a tough time paying back interest and principal to the bondholders. Bondholders sell their bonds in the secondary market. The price of the bonds drop and Joe is worried it could get worse. Joe sells his bond for $4000—$1000 less than he paid for it.

Advantages of Mutual Funds

You knew there were advantage—that's why you bought the book!

Mutual Funds Are Diversified

When you're investing in a mutual fund, you needn't worry so much that you might invest in one dud. As mentioned earlier, most funds own a large number of investments. In other words, they're diversified. If one investment owned by the fund performs poorly, there's still hope that the others might rally. At least, you're less likely to lose as much.

Technobabble

Diversified means funds are spread out among a large number of different investments. *Distributions* are dividends and capital gains distributed by mutual funds to their shareholders. *Interest income* represents earnings you receive from bonds and/or the fixed-income securities. *Capital gains* are profits on the sale of securities. A variety of funds available to investors from one investment management company may be known as a *fund family*.

Mutual fund regulations give you some added protection. They set a ten percent limit on your mutual fund's investment (up to a maximum of 20 percent within a fund family) in any one stock or bond issuer. Suppose a fund owns 50 different stocks, including Computer Chip Inc. One day there is terrible news about Computer Chip Inc., and the stock price drops five percent. That's a big loss for a stock! The other 49 stocks don't drop in price, however. In fact, some rise. At the end of the day, that Computer Chip Inc. loss didn't put a dent in the value of the fund.

Mutual funds also relieve you of a major workload. Who has time nowadays to play the stock market or find a company with a great credit record? Not only that, but by the time we peons hear about a great investment, it's generally too late to profit from it.

Enter mutual funds....

You Get Your Own Investment Pro

With a mutual fund, you get your own highly trained hired gun or guns working full-time to ensure that you make money. The fund manager, or portfolio manager, has all the investment research at his or her fingertips, and even visits companies before investing. This individual often earns a high salary plus a bonus at year's end if a fund performs better than similar funds. This gives the fund manager a high level of incentive to ensure that the fund does well. Some funds are managed by a team of portfolio managers.

Higher Returns on Your Investment Are Possible

With a mutual fund, you have greater potential to grow your money over the long term than you do in a bank. Deposit your money into a savings account today and earn less than one percent. Money market funds earn you significantly higher returns as they invest in high-yielding short-term debt instruments. The value of your mutual fund fluctuates with changing market conditions.

Mutual Funds Pay You Back

A mutual fund's earnings on its investments ultimately are passed on to you as *distributions*. There are three types of distributions you can receive from a fund. When the fund owns bonds, it earns interest income. When a fund owns stocks it may earn dividends. The dividends are a share of company profits that are paid periodically to its shareholders. When the fund sells either stock or bond investments at a profit, the profits are called capital gains. You can receive your distributions in cash, or you can have your mutual fund reinvest the money to buy more units in the fund.

You Get Your Money Whenever You Want It

You can buy and sell all or part of your mutual fund whenever you want. You generally can get your cash in a couple of days. In some cases, there may be redemption charges—check your fund prospectus.

You Have a Fund Family

Many mutual fund families offer investors a wide variety of mutual funds. The funds may invest in different kinds of stocks, bonds, or cash equivalents based on different investment objectives. When one investment company owns a number of mutual funds, those funds are considered part of a fund family. Some of the biggest mutual fund companies have over 30 different funds in their family. Mutual fund families make investing easy. Most fund companies allow you to switch from one fund to another, usually at no charge. This allows your portfolio to change as your money situation or the markets change.

You Don't Have to Be Rich to Invest

As we told you earlier, you don't need much money to invest in a mutual fund. Although you may need several thousand dollars to invest in individual stocks and bonds, you can get started in a mutual fund with as little as $25 through a monthly purchase plan. With lump-sum purchases of most funds, though, you need $500 to $1000. Minimums may be lower for RRSP accounts. When you open an account, you are on record as a unitholder of the fund. You get periodic statements from the

Hot Tip

Haven't got a chunk of money to invest? Set up a purchase plan for as little as $25 per month into the mutual fund of your choice. Contact your investment advisor for details.

fund showing how many shares of the fund you own, the distributions you have received, and how much your holdings in the fund are worth.

Mutual Funds Are Highly Regulated

Mutual funds are regulated by a variety of agencies, including the newly formed Mutual Fund Dealers Association, the Investment Funds Institute of Canada (IFIC), and the various provincial securities commissions. The funds are required to report their financial activities to these agencies. Meanwhile, mutual funds also are required to send unitholders financial reports. Often, reports are consolidated for a fund group or family. Therefore, if you own more than one mutual fund in a fund group or family, you won't necessarily have to keep track of a hundred different pieces of paper.

Sidelines

Even if the company managing a fund bites the dust, no creditor will have access to your investment. Your assets are deposited in an account in your name at a custodian, which is responsible for the safekeeping of your account. The fund group can't touch your account.

You Can Save for Your Retirement

Mutual funds are a great way to save for retirement. On your application to open your mutual fund account, you merely arrange to have it set up as a Registered Retirement Savings Plan (RRSP). With this retirement plan, which you learn more about in Chapter 19, you not only get the benefits of mutual fund investment profits, but also get to deduct annual contributions from your income on your tax return. Meanwhile, you pay no taxes on your earnings until you retire. Not a bad deal!

You Get Automatic Investment and Withdrawals

You know how you can have your paycheque automatically sent by your employer to your chequing account? You can do the same with your mutual fund. As little as $25 a month can be automatically taken out of your chequing account and invested in your mutual fund. If you're retired and need income, you also can arrange to receive

Hot Tip

Check with your employer to see if they offer any benefits that may complement your RRSP strategy. They may contribute money to your RRSP plan at no cost to you or they may allow you to purchase their stock if you work for a public company (usually at a reduced price).

Look Out!

Unlike a CDIC-insured bank GIC, you're not guaranteed to receive your original investment, or *principal*, back with a mutual fund. So, before investing, it's critical to investigate the quality of a mutual fund's investments.

monthly payments from your mutual fund, in addition to having your mutual fund automatically reinvest distributions to buy more units in your fund. You also can arrange to invest the distributions of one fund automatically into another fund, provided that it is in the same family.

The Least You Need to Know

➤ The kinds of securities a mutual fund invests in affect the value of the mutual fund.

➤ Mutual funds invest in either stocks, bonds, or cash equivalents. Some invest in all three.

➤ With stocks, you own a piece of a company. You can quickly make a lot of money, but you also can lose big.

➤ Bonds are like loans to companies or governments.

➤ Even if you invest in high-quality bonds, you can lose if you're not careful. If interest rates head up, the bond price falls, so you can suffer a loss of much of your original investment if you sell. A bond's interest payments don't increase when interest rates do. You will, however, get your principal back upon maturity if the issuer does not default.

➤ Mutual funds are diversified. They own a large number of securities. If you have one dud in your mutual fund, the others still can rally.

➤ Mutual funds also offer professional management.

Chapter 4

Mutual Funds for Everyone

> **In This Chapter**
>
> ➤ Mutual funds come in several flavours
>
> ➤ Spotting a fund with a good batting average
>
> ➤ Investing in mutual funds for a long time

As someone once said, there's a mutual fund for all seasons. To help zero in on the right fund or funds for you, you first need to know which categories to examine.

Would you like a fund that takes risks in the hopes of big gains? Do you want a fund that invests in small companies or a fund that invests in large companies? Do you want a fund that invests overseas?

There also are funds specifically for the more squeamish investor that enable you to earn a decent return on investment with little risk. Part 3 of this book discusses in more detail the different types of mutual funds and the investments they make. In this chapter, you get acquainted with the different ways mutual funds are classified.

What Flavour Is Your Fund?

Now that you know about the inside of mutual funds, you're ready to get to the real meat of the matter—the funds themselves. As we mentioned before, there are more mutual funds than you can shake a stick at. Before you can determine which mutual funds are right for you (more about that later in Part 2), you need to review the menu.

Sidelines

Different types of funds pay different types of distributions, so your need for regular income is an important key to determining what type of fund you select. Chapter 3 presents all the different kinds of distributions—dividends from stocks, interest income from bonds, and capital gains from the fund's sale of either stock or bond securities at a profit.

The type of fund you select determines the distributions you get, if any. For example, stock fund distributions may come from capital gains and from dividends. A bond fund distribution also may come from capital gains. In addition, bond fund distributions come from interest income. Some funds, such as balanced funds, own both stocks and bonds. They may pay distributions from all three sources—dividends, capital gains, and interest income.

It's easy to find mutual funds that invest in any one of the securities we discussed in Chapter 3—stocks, bonds, or cash—or a mishmash of any of these securities.

Mutual funds might invest in stocks of one particular type of company. Some specialize, for example, in small companies. There also are funds for middle-size companies and some for larger companies.

Certain funds invest in companies based in one particular type of industry, such as health sciences or technology. Still others invest in companies that mine gold bullion. It's also possible a fund could invest in the stocks or bonds of companies overseas.

Whenever you're considering a mutual fund, it's important first to pin down a mutual fund's investment objective. Fund objectives tell you exactly what the fund manager hopes to accomplish with your money. For example, "the fund provides a steady flow of income with reasonable safety of capital and liquidity" or "long-term capital growth by investing in mid-sized Canadian companies."

Often the fund objective is smack-dab in the fund's name, but to double-check, always locate the fund objective in the fund's prospectus. You can also double-check with your broker or investment advisor.

It's only by learning about a fund's investment objective that you can determine whether it matches your own.

Look for These Clues

Now, put on your Sherlock Holmes hat and get out your magnifying glass. You're going to learn how to decipher what's in a mutual fund and what it all means.

Please note that the average annual returns of the fund groups discussed in the next sections are based on average annual returns over the ten years ending in 1997, according to BellCharts.

Clue No. 1: Growth

See the word "growth" in the name or investment objective of a mutual fund, and chances are that fund investments largely are in stocks. By growth, we mean that fund is designed to register big increases in the share price. You also may be in for a roller-coaster ride because the fund's share price can go up and down. Based on historical performance, investors tend to make great profits with growth funds over the long term, but they also risk losing the most. Funds with the word "growth" in the fund objective are apt to fall into one of the following categories:

Look Out!

Invest in an aggressive-growth, growth, small-company or sector fund for just one or two years, and you could lose your shirt! Over the past 50 years, the worst return for speculative stock funds was -27 percent. In 1973 and 1974, the average stock fund lost a total of 45 percent.

➤ *Aggressive growth funds,* also known as *small-cap funds,* are among the most speculative funds. The fund manager invests mostly in smaller companies. Small companies plow profits back into the company to grow their businesses and hope to become larger outfits. This is what you bank on as an investor. Typically, there are fewer shares of a small company traded. As a result, small company stock prices can be volatile. Although these funds have the potential to give you very large returns on your investment, they

Sidelines

Stock fund portfolio managers use different strategies that they hope will make their shareholders richer. There are two basic investment styles that are used to select stocks.

Stock funds that buy on *value* tend to invest in overlooked stocks that appear as if they could increase in price. The funds gain when the companies register unexpected profits and other investors start buying the stock in droves. By contrast, fund managers who invest for *growth* want to own companies whose earnings are growing rapidly, often at more than 25 to 30 percent or more a year.

Does it matter which style a fund manager uses? Over ten-year periods, there has been little difference in the returns on funds that invest for growth or value. However, over a shorter period, three months to three years, for example, it is possible for one investment style to outperform the other. You can hedge your bets by owning both types of stock funds, investing for growth and value, or you can stick with one style and invest regularly for the long term.

also can rack up the heaviest losses. Aggressive stock funds as a group delivered an average annual return of 10.6 percent over the past ten years.

➤ *Growth funds,* which are less risky than aggressive growth funds, invest in the stocks of companies that have been around for a while and should be profitable for years to come. Typically, these are the larger and mid-sized companies with good, steady track records. Over the long haul, these funds have the potential to appreciate in value. Over the past 10 years, long-term growth funds as a group have delivered an average 10.8 percent annual return.

➤ *Dividend Funds* invest in blue-chip stocks that provide long-term growth and pay regular dividends. Blue-chip companies are the larger, established companies that tend to have solid earnings and less potential for appreciation in value. They offer less risk compared to regular growth funds, and they offer a steady stream of income. Dividend funds have averaged an 11.1 percent return over the past ten years.

➤ *Specialty funds,* also known as *sector funds,* invest in the stock of one specific industry. These funds generally are among the riskiest because the fund manager puts all the eggs in one basket. Not all specialty funds are alike; some are riskier than others. There are specialty funds that focus their investments on financial services, health care, real estate, resources, technology, and so forth. These funds can be high-risk gambits. Investors can earn whopping returns on investment or they can lose their shirts if they invest at the wrong time. For example, the average technology stock fund delivered a 12.5 percent annual return rate over the past ten years.

➤ Gold and precious metals are another popular type of specialty fund. Gold and precious metals, such as platinum and silver, tend to soar in value when the prices for necessities rise. For that reason, some investors routinely keep a little money in gold funds. Recall that in the late 1970s, when the price of oil shot up 40 percent, the price of gold also hit $800 an ounce. Mutual funds that invested in gold mining stocks gained a whopping 100 percent! Gold funds, however, are volatile investments and can lose big when the prices of goods and services stagnate or fall. Over the past ten years, gold funds as a group experienced an average annual return of 4.3 percent.

Clue No. 2: Income

The word "income" in the name or investment objective of the fund means the fund pays periodic income or interest. These funds tend to be less risky than growth or aggressive growth funds because the periodic income helps make up for any future potential declines. Be prepared, though, for lower overall returns long-term than you might get with a growth or aggressive-growth fund. You normally do not get the increase in share price and thus increase in the value of the investment that you would get from investing in aggressive growth or growth stock funds.

Don't be surprised if your mutual fund salesperson calls this type of fund a *fixed-income* fund even though you can't necessarily find those exact words in the fund's investment objective. Fixed-income fund is another term for a bond fund. Bond funds are considered less-risky mutual funds because bondholders have first priority for payoff if a company goes under. However, as we mention in Chapter 13, these funds can rise and fall in value as interest rates fluctuate. Inflation also can erode the purchasing power of the money. The average ten-year annual return for a Canadian bond fund was 9.9 percent.

In this chapter, we've explored primarily stock funds. Of course, there are different bond mutual funds to sift through as well. Recall that bond funds may invest all or part of their money in issues of corporations, foreign governments, or domestic governments

Technobabble

Income refers to periodic interest or dividend distributions from a fund. *Growth* means long-term appreciation in value as a result of increases in share price. *Blue-chip* stocks are issued by well-established companies that typically pay a dividend. *Equity* is another word for stock.

Sidelines

Some stock funds pay very little, if anything, in the way of distributions. Small company or aggressive stock funds, for example, don't distribute much dividend income to shareholders at all. Why? These funds invest in smaller companies that are busy pumping all their profits back into their businesses. A fund, however, that invests in small company stocks may own each stock for a relatively short period of time, potentially producing capital gain distributions, so it's possible for a small company stock fund to produce capital gains.

Most mutual funds distribute income from interest monthly and income from stock dividends every three months. Capital gains are distributed once a year, usually in December. You can find out when a fund pays distributions by reading the fund's prospectus, which you will learn about in Chapter 9.

When you open an account to invest in a mutual fund, you have a choice. You can elect to receive the distributions from the fund as cash or have the fund reinvest the distributions into new units of your existing fund. If you don't need the income, it's generally best to reinvest.

(federal, provincial, or municipal). Both Canadian federal and provincial government-bond-based mutual funds are considered among the least-risky bond funds as they are backed by the full faith of the Canadian government. High-yield bond funds are considered among the more-risky bond funds as they consist of mostly lower-grade quality corporate bonds. (Corporate bonds are considered riskier investments because the risk of a corporation defaulting on payment is much greater than it would be with the Canadian government.) To compensate the investor for the additional credit risk, these funds offer higher yields, hence the name *high-yield*.

The longer the bond fund's term, the greater your chances of losing money if interest rates rise (see Chapter 3). Of course, on the upside, when interest rates fall, bond prices rise. Chapters 12 and 13 take a closer look at bond fund categories that may be right for you based on your income needs and tolerance for risk. Chapter 13 also takes a closer look at why long-term bond funds show greater changes in price when interest rates change.

In most cases, you won't get the capital appreciation from a bond fund that you get from a stock fund over the long term. These funds are designed to pay investors semi-annual or monthly income.

Balanced Funds

Balanced funds bridge the gap between stock funds and bond funds; that is, they split their investments relatively equally between stocks and bonds. These funds provide both growth and income by investing in both stocks (usually blue-chip) and government and/or high-quality corporate bonds. Some funds, however, may invest 10 percent to 15 percent of their money in small company or foreign stocks. Balanced funds are less risky than stock funds but a little more risky than certain bond funds. For example, balanced funds have experienced an average annual return of 10.3 percent over the past ten years. You might not necessarily find the word "balanced" in the title of these types of funds, so you'll have to check the fund's investment objective.

International Funds

International funds invest in stocks or bonds worldwide. There are a wide variety of international funds to pick from—international growth, growth and income, and small company stock funds. There are funds that invest in a specific region of the world such as the United States, Europe, Asia, or Latin America. For example, the average U.S. equity fund delivered an annual ten-year return of 14.6 percent. Then there are funds that invest in a single country. Some funds invest worldwide, excluding Canada or North America. Those funds that invest in both Canada and foreign countries are known as *global funds* or *world funds*.

The more countries a fund invests in, the less risky it is. That's because the financial markets of different countries don't always move the same way. When the Japanese market may be dropping in value, the European markets may be moving higher. As a result, losses in one country may be offset by gains in another. Over the past ten years, foreign funds have grown at an average annual rate of 10.9 percent.

Regional funds or *single-country funds* are riskier than diversified international funds—all your eggs are in one basket. Your fortune may rise and fall within one country or area of the world. If there is a political uprising in the Far East, for example, the Asian stock markets may tumble. If one country, such as Japan, falls on economic tough times, Japan-fund investors can lose investment value.

Regional or single-country fund investing can be a boom-or-bust proposition. Over the past ten years, for example, the funds that invested in the countries of the Pacific Basin had an average annual return of 14.8 percent, according to Morningstar (based on ten-year annual return ending, 1994).

There are funds that invest in corporate and government bonds worldwide. These are the least risky of the international-bond fund groups.

Someone who invests in international bond funds should not expect to earn a whopping amount more than they would by investing here at home. Bond funds that invest world-wide, for example, had an average annual total return of 9.8 percent over the past ten years. By contrast, on average, Canadian bond funds gained 9.9 percent over the same period. However, by investing in international bond funds, you get diversification.

Hot Tip

Total assets under management in money market funds in Canada were over $32 billion as of April 1998.

For Even Less Risky Returns...

As we told you in Chapter 3, money market funds invest mostly in money market or cash-equivalent investments—typically short-term government and company debt. These tend to be lower yielding, and have lower total returns, but they are less risky than the other types of funds described earlier in this chapter. Another type of money market fund is a T-bill fund, or Treasury Bill fund, which invests only in Government of Canada debt with maturities of usually less than a year. T-bill funds usually earn

Hot Tip

The first Canadian mutual fund was established more than 60 years ago. Today, fund companies manage over $176 billion in assets! There are over 1800 mutual funds available to suit your particular objectives.

less for the investor, but are considered less risky than money market funds.

The Least You Need to Know

➤ Some mutual funds aim for growth in the value of your investment; others may aim for income from interest and dividends.

➤ Bond funds or fixed-income funds pay you income. They may invest both in Canada and abroad.

➤ Balanced funds invest in both stock and bonds for more conservative investors.

Chapter 5

Is a Fund a Winner or Loser?

In This Chapter

➤ Betting on the *right* mutual fund

➤ Deciphering those performance figures

➤ Knowing what the averages are

Before you invest in a mutual fund, you need to act like a schoolteacher and give it a cool, objective evaluation. Once you know the ABCs, you can make a solid lifetime investment.

Where to Get the Risk Information

To evaluate a fund, you first have to know what to look for and what all this financial stuff means. There are several measurements to determine how well a fund has performed and what you can expect to earn today.

You can get information about a fund's total return, yield, and measures of risk, which are discussed later in this chapter, from several sources of information, including the fund's prospectus, local newspaper mutual fund tables, or papers such as *The Globe and Mail* or *The Financial Post*. Chapters 9 and 10 show you how to find all the information you need to make wise investment decisions.

Then, once you finally invest, it's important to keep your eye on the ball. In this chapter, you'll learn how to monitor your mutual funds' performance.

What's a Fund's Batting Average?

Chances are you can figure out that a baseball player with 25 home runs and a .350 batting average will be named to the All Star team.

Just think if you had the same insight in advance about your mutual fund! There's no reason why you can't if you simply check on how a mutual fund is doing *before* you buy it. You certainly don't want to bet on a loser.

Luckily, you don't have to be Albert Einstein to figure things out. The rest of this chapter explains the basic ways to evaluate funds. More detailed evaluations are explained in later chapters.

Check Out the Yield

There are a lot of numbers associated with mutual funds, and it's important to be sure you're comparing apples to apples.

As discussed in Chapter 3, a mutual fund pays distributions based on dividend income from stocks, interest income from bonds, and capital gains from the profitable sale of both.

The yield, expressed as a percentage of the fund's current net asset value or price per unit, tells how much income you get from these sources. It measures the interest income, in the case of bonds, or dividend income, in the case of stock funds. This figure is particularly useful if you need to have steady money coming in. It allows you to compare the periodic income each fund generates.

The yield is expressed as an annual number—it represents a yield for a full 12 months. Suppose, for example, a fund paid out 60 cents in dividends for the year and the fund's net asset value is $10. Sixty cents divided by ten equals six percent.

Hot Tip

Canadian mutual funds have been around for decades, but they have only been actively rated over the past ten years. Business papers such as *The Financial Post* and *The Globe and Mail* offer mutual fund publications. If you have access to the Internet, all of the major fund companies have Web sites.

Check Out Operating Expenses—They Can Cost You

Fund expenses are taken out before the mutual fund distributes income or dividends. Like any company, the mutual fund must pay for the normal cost of doing business—including, for example, costs associated with the management of the fund, custody of the fund's assets, and servicing of the fund's unitholders. These operating expenses are not paid directly by the investor. They are paid by the fund from its assets before distributions are made to the investor. The higher the operating expenses the fund has, the lower the amount of distributions to shareholders. Chapter 8 discusses mutual fund costs in greater detail.

The Total Return

In a mutual fund, you don't only profit from distributions in the form of interest and dividends. You also stand to make money if the market price of your mutual fund rises. Total return reflects all these figures.

What good is it to invest in a high-yielding fund only to find that the market value of the investment has dropped? Total return measures how well the fund is doing overall. If a fund manager is making the right investments, buying the right securities, adjusting the fund's investments to avoid large losses, and letting the profits roll in, the fund will have a positive total return.

Simply put, total return represents the change in the fund's unit price plus the amount of money generated from reinvested income and capital gains distributions. Divide this by the original share price to calculate your total return rate.

You don't need to worry about fund expenses when you calculate the total return. As mentioned previously, the mutual fund deducts expenses before paying you distributions. As a result, the fund's yield already reflects the expenses that were taken out.

If you only know that the total return of a fund over three years is 52 percent, you're stuck! That doesn't tell you the average annual return. You have to do some complicated algebra (to factor in compounding) to come up with this number, which, by the way, is 15 percent. But, don't worry—most newspapers and mutual fund reporting services (discussed in Chapter 10) list the annual average returns.

Check Out the Fund's Long-Term Batting Average

Got the hang of it? A good fund has a good long-term batting average but, over the short term, like a baseball player, the fund can have some off years.

Perhaps a fund manager had a bad case of the hiccups in 1995. That doesn't necessarily mean you give up your Mickey Mantle or Hank Aaron of the mutual fund world. In Chapter 6 you will learn to pick the funds that are right for you based on your investment comfort level.

Look Out!

When comparing returns on mutual funds, make sure you're comparing apples with apples. You want to be comparing funds in the same category with similar objectives. Obviously, a higher-risk-type fund such as a resource fund will produce dramatically different returns from a low-risk money market fund.

With all this talk about total returns and the growth in the share value of mutual fund investments, what could an investor expect to earn over the long term? Past performance is no indication of future returns, but can give us an indication as to the volatility of the fund. To help zero in on your mutual fund choices, compare the average annual returns over the long term.

Gauging a Fund's Risk

There are a couple of easy ways to figure out how risky a fund is. The more volatile a fund, the greater chance you'll see wide swings in the return and unit value of a fund. The swing in performance as measured by the fund's total return is known as *volatility*. In bad years, a volatile fund will lose a lot more money than other funds. However, in good years you can see double-digit returns.

How Did a Fund Do in Bad Years?

There's a relatively easy way to gauge a stock fund's risk. Compare how a number of stock funds did in bad years, such as 1973, 1974, 1981, 1987, 1990, and 1994. Suppose you're seriously considering three stock funds and they've all performed about the same. Here's what to consider:

> Growth Stock Fund A has grown at an annual rate of 13.25 percent over the past ten years, stock Fund B gained 12.98 percent, and C was up 13.4 percent.

Compare the funds' returns in 1987, 1990, and 1994.

How to Gauge a Bond Fund's Risks of Losing Money

There are a couple of ways to tell whether a bond fund is too hot to handle. These measures, duration and average maturity, can help you assess the riskiness of a bond fund.

As discussed in Chapter 3, bond prices move in the opposite direction as interest rates. When interest rates rise, prices for bonds fall. By contrast, when interest rates fall, prices for bonds rise.

Duration measures how much your bond fund will increase or decrease in value with a one percent change in interest rates. A fund with a duration of four, for example, drops about four percent in value if interest rates rise one percent, but it increases four percent in value if interest rates drop one percent. By contrast, a fund with a duration of ten loses ten percent in value if interest rates rise one percent, but increases ten percent in value if interest rates drop one percent.

There's another easy way to measure a bond fund's risk: look at its *average maturity*. The lower the average maturity, the less money the fund loses when interest rates rise. The higher the average maturity, the more money the bond fund loses if interest rates increase. By contrast, the higher the average maturity, the more the bond fund will make if interest rates fall.

Bond mutual funds typically own a lot of different bonds that mature in different years. How do you tell the average maturity of the bonds owned by a bond fund? Check the fund prospectus or consult your investment advisor.

Tips on Spotting a Winning Fund

Chapter 16 will show you how to evaluate a fund or several funds' performances after you already own them. You will learn when to dump the losers and keep the winners.

The Least You Need to Know

➤ When shopping for mutual funds:

➤ Understand the fund objective.

➤ Compare a fund's annual returns over at least three, five, and ten years. (Be sure you're comparing similar funds, e.g., growth funds with growth funds).

➤ Read the fund prospectus and/or consult with your investment advisor.

➤ Check how the fund did in bad years.

➤ Don't choose the funds with the hottest short-term track records. Last year's winners could be this year's laggards.

➤ Find out who the fund's portfolio manager is. Make sure the person responsible for a fund's strong track record is still running the show.

Part 2
Getting Started

Now we're getting serious, folks. The most important part of mutual fund investing is in the coming chapters. Remember, before you fill out the application, you need to make sure you're picking the right funds.

Don't worry—you don't need an MBA to do this. All you need are a few tricks. Believe it or not, the key to mutual fund investing is not necessarily knowing any major secrets about the direction of interest rates or major industry trends. It's knowing yourself and then knowing what to look for based on your own unique nature.

We're not talking major brain surgery here, so just sit back in a comfortable chair and relax. Consider this the matchmaking part of the book. It will help you figure out your own personal investment profile and steer you in the direction of funds that may be right for you.

JIM'S HERE FOR THE BIG INVESTMENTS. LARRY FOR OUR SMALLER PROPERTIES.

Chapter 6

What Kind of Investor Are You?

In This Chapter

➤ The risks of investing in mutual funds

➤ How much risk can you tolerate?

➤ What type of investor are you?

Are you ready to invest? On your mark, get set... stop!

Stock and bond prices can bounce up and down a lot. Are you *really* ready? Pick up the business section of your local newspaper any day of the week and you'll see what we mean. Sure, you might be inspired because of a newspaper and magazine report that some mutual fund investors are making big profits. Wow! ABC mutual fund gained 20 percent so far this year. Joe Biddle invested $1000 and now six months later it's up to $1200! Then again, none of us needs to get burned by investing our life savings in a hot stock fund only to have it nosedive over the following few weeks.

Although you now have a clear picture of your savings goals and how to free the money to invest, that's not enough.

You have to be sure you understand what you're getting into before committing your hard-earned cash to anything that fails to move consistently in a northerly direction.

That's why we're here, so read on....

What Are Ya in For?

Unfortunately, there are some pain-in-the-neck risks you need to contend with when you invest in mutual funds. The one that's most likely to trigger a headache is losing money. You also can make a killing, however. Your success as a mutual fund investor depends largely on how you handle the downside of this otherwise attractive investment.

Take John and Mary, who just retired to sunny West Palm Beach, Florida. They live on John's pension and some savings. Before John retired, he put the bulk of their life savings—$25,000—in a growth-oriented mutual fund.

Three months later, the value of his fund had plunged $3000. Before John had time to regret his investment decision, he managed to crack his tooth while eating dinner at a local restaurant.

Because he had no dental insurance, he was forced to spend $3000 for a bridge. He had to sell his mutual fund at precisely the wrong time.

That's what we mean by risk—investing in a mid- to high-risk mutual fund when you really can't afford to lose.

What's risky for John and Mary, however, may not be risky for somebody else.

Tad, a 35-year-old dentist, makes 100 grand a year. Tad is comfortable investing in growth-oriented mutual funds because he is aware that the $10,000 he invested today can drop in value over the short term. But he also knows that mutual funds are great investments for the long term. Tad has a good job. He can afford to invest for 25 to 30 years and build a nest egg. He won't be upset if his $10,000 investment is worth $9000 at the end of this year because there's a good chance it could be worth $12,000 at the end of the following year.

There are a few reasons a mutual fund can fall in value. We already discussed some of these in Chapter 3. Mutual funds invest generally in stocks, bonds, or both. When tons of investors all over the country buy stocks, stock prices head up. If those same investors sell stocks, stock prices can take a dive. Because a mutual fund may own the stocks all these investors are buying or selling, the value of a fund changes based on what these people do. You should make sure that your investment decisions take into account anticipated market trends.

Hot Tip

Mutual funds are long-term investments. The longer you invest, the less chance you have of losing. Based on financial history, stocks never have lost money over any 20-year period, according to Ibbotson Associates, Chicago. If you invest for just one year, you could lose money close to one-third of the time. Invest for five years and expect at least one bad year. This will give you a good idea of why it's important to invest in stock funds for the long term.

Believe it or not, there's also a risk that your investment can be *too* safe. Stay in an CDIC-insured savings account, for example, and your money may not grow fast enough to keep up with the prices of food and utilities. This is known as *inflation.*

True, your bank account is federally insured. You can't lose any money if your friendly banker goes out of business. Have you checked the interest banks pay on savings accounts, though? Rates are currently less than two percent!

What good is it if a few years down the road, you live on an investment that makes 100 bucks a week, but it costs $104 for groceries? You still have to reach into your pocketbook because you are $4 short.

Suppose you're saving for your child's university education. The cost of university is rising about six percent a year, and you estimate you need $100,000 for four years of tuition, room and board at Money Bags U. in 18 years.

If you earn too little on your child's university savings kitty and it grows to $85,000, you're in the hole. Where are you going to get the rest of the money?

Now, we don't want you to get overly upset about these Chicken Little stories. As mentioned at the beginning of the book, mutual fund managers are fully aware of these bugaboos and take steps to limit losses.

Hot Tip

Over the past 20 years, stock mutual funds have been the best way to beat inflation. Bond mutual funds have come in second.

Technobabble

Conservative investors like less-risky investments that lose little money. *Moderate investors* are willing to see the value of their mutual funds drop slightly in return for long-term profits. *Aggressive investors* want to earn big gains, but also are willing to accept big losses.

Zeroing in on Your Comfort Level

By asking yourself a few basic questions, you'll develop a better idea of the risk you're willing to assume when investing in mutual funds. You'll learn whether you're a conservative investor or a risk-taker. You don't want to invest in risky funds if you are a safety-minded investor. By the same token, if you like to invest aggressively, conservative funds aren't for you. Once you have this information in hand, you can move on to Chapter 7 to explore the kinds of mutual funds that fit your risk profile. You'll also learn how to divide your investments.

Risk-Tolerance Quiz

To help determine your risk tolerance, circle the letter that best expresses your answer to the following questions.

1. How old are you?

A. Over age 65 (1)

B. Between age 55 and 65 (2)

C. Between age 35 and 55 (3)

D. Under age 35 (4)

2. How much are you willing to lose in mutual fund investments in any given year?

A. One percent (1)

B. Three percent (2)

C. Ten percent (3)

D. 15 percent (4)

3. How important is regular income from your investments (that is, do you need to use the interest and dividends from your investments to cover expenses now)?

A. Very important (1)

B. Important (2)

C. Somewhat important (3)

D. Not important (4)

4. What is your time horizon (how long will the money be invested)?

A. Zero to two years (1)

B. Two to four years (2)

C. Four to six years (3)

D. More than six years (4)

5. How important is it to avoid losses and know your money is safe?

A. Very important (1)

B. Important (2)

C. Somewhat important (3)

D. Not important (4)

6. How important is it that your money grow faster than the prices you pay for the things you need?

   A. Not as important as getting regular income (1)

   B. I want it to grow as fast as the cost of things I need (2)

   C. I want it to grow more than the cost of things (3)

   D. I want it to grow much faster than the cost of things (4)

Now add up the numbers in parentheses to the right of each of your answers to determine your total risk-tolerance score:

➤ If your score is ten or less, you are a conservative investor. This means that safety is as important as seeing your money grow in value over the years.

➤ If you score between ten and 20, you are a moderate investor. You are willing to see your mutual funds decline in value a little bit in return for long-term growth.

➤ If you score 20 or more, you are an aggressive investor. You are willing to accept larger short-term losses than most people in return for substantial long-term gains.

This was just one fast and easy way to give you an idea of the type of investor you may be. It's always a good idea to consult with an investment advisor to evaluate your needs.

The Least You Need to Know

➤ Mutual funds can lose money.

➤ The money you make on your savings or mutual funds should grow at least as fast as the prices of food and other necessities.

➤ Before you invest, understand what kind of risk-taker you are.

eenie, meenie, miny, moe...

Chapter 7

Which Funds Are Right for You?

In This Chapter

➤ Matching your tolerance for risk with the right funds

➤ How to split up your investments

➤ Avoiding common fund-selection mistakes

➤ How to avoid funds that are too risky

You might consider this chapter the Culinary Institute of Mutual Funds. You have the ingredients lined up: how much risk you can stand, how much money you need by when, and the types of mutual funds from which to select. Now you're going to mix it all together.

The general rule is: the higher the yield in the case of bond funds or the higher the total return in the case of stock funds, the more risky the mutual fund. (Unfortunately, even the most savvy investors can't necessarily have everything!) Investing for the long term is key to reaping any benefits from an aggressive or growth-oriented mutual fund. Invest for a year or two and you can lose. Investors with just a couple of years to invest also need to protect what they have in less-risky investments.

This chapter takes what you already learned about yourself and mutual funds and helps put it into a format to help meet your needs. You'll see which funds are for which types of investors. You'll also discover how to split your money among different types of funds to get the best return with the least amount of risk.

You already know how much heat you can stand. The time has come to select the funds that match your risk tolerance. If you took the short quiz in Chapter 6, you now know whether you are an aggressive, moderate, or conservative investor. You know how much you can stomach losing in a year's time in return for the long-term profits. You also know whether anything short of an CDIC-insured investment makes you queasy.

Let's take a minute to review the investments available. Think of investing in funds based on a pyramid of risk, such as the one illustrated in this chapter. At the top are the riskiest funds, the funds that can lose or gain a lot of money over a short time. The riskiest funds often pay the highest returns. For instance, funds that invest in just one sector of an industry can gain 70 percent or lose 30 percent in any given year.

Next in line, in level of risk, are aggressive-growth funds and small company stock funds. You also can win big or lose a lot with these. Although speculators often move in and out of aggressive growth and small company stock funds, they also are excellent long-term investments. Sock money into one of these babies for 20 years and you could have a nice retirement nest egg.

Next in line are growth funds, which also are considered good investments for the long term. These funds tend to invest in larger, well-established companies, but they also can be risky.

There are many well-managed growth funds to pick. Moderate and conservative

Figure 7.1
Pyramid of Risk

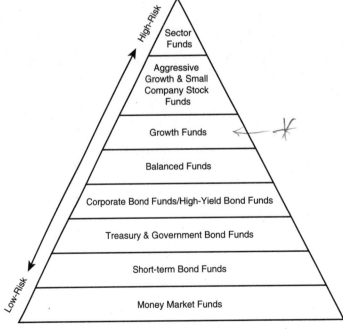

investors may look at the middle of the investment pyramid. Balanced funds are sleep-at-night stock funds. You can get rich slowly and with relative low risk with these funds.

Corporate bond (also known as high-yield bond) funds are next on the pyramid. You'll earn higher yields, but typically you won't get the kind of growth you get from stock funds. Funds that invest in Treasury bonds are less risky than their corporate counterparts because the bonds are backed against default by the government. At the bottom of the pyramid are the least-risky funds—short-term bond funds and money market funds.

If you have a short-term investment time span, it's best to stick with the lowest-risk funds.

Matchmaker, Matchmaker, Make Me a Match

Investing in mutual funds is a long-term affair. Pick out the right types of funds and you can stick with them for life. The key to choosing mutual funds is to find the fund that matches your objectives and risk tolerance. To help you along, let's first learn what *not* to do.

Avoid a Fistful of Mistakes

Make yourself happy by picking the right funds. Unfortunately—and you've probably heard all too many of these horror stories—many mutual fund investors don't. Don't make the same mistakes.

1. **Don't chase after the hot funds.** Once you read about a hot fund with a sizzling return in the newspaper or a personal finance magazine, it's usually too late to invest!

2. **Don't invest to make a quick profit.** Do that and you could lose big. Mutual funds, on the whole, should be a long-term investment.

3. **Don't chase after high yields.** Remember, the higher the yield, the greater the risk. When comparing a short-, intermediate-, or long-term bond fund to its respective group averages, be suspicious if a fund outyields similar funds by a wide margin. Suppose the average long-term bond fund yields seven percent and you are looking at a specific long-term bond fund that yields more than ten percent. The fund that yields over 10 percent is high-risk. How else could the fund pay those yields?

4. **Don't play it too safe.** T-bills and money market funds are good short-term places to park your money. If you're socking away money for your retirement, however, stock funds historically have been a better deal for the long term.

5. **Don't pick unsuitable funds.** If you need income and lower risk, you should not be investing in aggressive stock funds.

6. **Don't pick a fund based on its name alone, rather than checking on the actual securities the fund buys.** Some funds have more flexibility than others to invest in different kinds of stocks or bonds. You can't always tell by the name of the fund.

7. **Don't panic and sell when the market goes down.** Remember, you're in it for the long term.

Getting a Good Fit

Try wearing the wrong size shoes for a day and see how you feel; there's nothing worse for your lovely disposition. The same goes for mutual funds. Chapter 4 discussed the different kinds of funds in which you can invest. Now let's try on a fund for size. Table 7.1 ranks stock and bond funds by their risk level, as well as the potential for the following types of rewards:

➤ "Big gains" refer to potential for very high total returns because the objective of the fund is to speculate for the purpose of rapid and large increases in the share value of the fund.

➤ "Maximum growth" refers to the potential of producing the highest total returns from funds that invest most aggressively in stocks.

➤ "Growth" refers to higher-than-average total returns because the funds invest in stocks for long-term growth in the share value of the fund.

➤ "Income" refers to the potential ability of the fund to provide investors with regular interest and/or dividends.

➤ "Low risk" and "least risk" refer to the potential capability of the fund to preserve your principal.

Getting the Best Returns with the Least Amount of Risk

There is one more step to nailing down your mutual fund investments. Once you know your risk level, you can invest in different types of funds so that you can get the best possible return with the least risk.

Diversification Helps Limit Losses

Earlier in this book, we told you that the major advantage of mutual funds is that they diversify their investments. They might, for example, buy stocks of several different companies. This way, if one performs poorly, the others might not. Gurus say

Table 7.1 Getting Comfortable with a Fund

Investor Risk Level/Objective	Type of Fund	Risk/Reward
Stock Funds		
Speculative	Precious metals	Highest/Big gains
Speculative	Most sector	Higher/Big gains
Aggressive	Aggressive growth/ Small company	High/Maximum capital growth
Aggressive	International growth	High/Maximum capital growth
Aggressive	Growth	High/Longer-term growth
Conservative	Income	Lower/Long-term income
Conservative	Balanced	Lower/Income and growth
Bond Funds		
Aggressive	High-yield	High/High income
Moderate	Long-term government	Moderate/Income
Aggressive	International	High/Income
Moderate	Intermediate-term	Moderate/Income
Conservative	Short-term	Lower/Income and less risk
Other Funds		
Safety-minded	Money market	Lowest/Income and least risk

it could pay to take a similar strategy when you pick your mutual funds. They call this diversification.

Diversification means that if you divide your investments the right way, gains in one type of mutual fund can offset losses in other types of funds.

Look at it this way. Suppose you're graphing the performance of a couple of mutual funds. Over several years, Fund A's performance looks just like an M. It goes up and it goes down. Fund B's performance looks like a W. It goes down, then up, then down and back up again.

If you own just one of these funds, you're in for a wild ride. Put them together and you get an entirely different picture. Losses in one fund are offset by gains in the other. You get a less bumpy ride.

Slicing Up Your Investment Pie

How do you know how many of your available investment dollars to invest in each kind of mutual fund? One easy way to figure it out is to subtract your age from 100; the number you get is how much to invest in stocks. If you are 40 years old, 100 - 40 = 60. Based on this calculation, you put 60 percent of your money in stocks and 40 percent in bonds and money market funds. Again, this calculation provides a very rough idea of how to break down your investments and should not serve as a hard-and-fast rule, as you'll see in the next section. Your stockbroker or investment advisor also can help you find the best mix of funds.

Technobabble

When you *diversify* your mutual fund investments, you own different kinds of funds so that losses in one fund can be offset by gains in the others. Diversification is designed to give you the best returns with the least possible risk. *Hedging* is selecting investments so that the losses in one or more investments are offset by gains in others and vice versa. To hedge, you look for investments that perform at odds with each other. When one is gaining value, the other is losing value, and vice versa.

Figure 7.2
How Diversification Works to Smooth Out the Bumps.

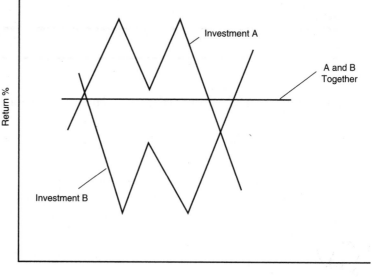

The Main Ingredients

You need four major ingredients to diversify your mutual fund recipe:

➤ **Stock funds.** Invest in stock funds for growth and inflation protection. Recall that stocks historically have earned six to seven percent more than the rate of inflation.

➤ **Bond funds.** Invest in bond funds for income and to hedge against stock fund losses. Stock fund and bond fund prices don't always move in the same direction, so if you own a bond fund, it could cushion the blow of losses in your stock funds or other investments.

➤ **Money market funds.** Money funds generally are a stabilizer and, when interest rates rise, you earn higher yields from a money market fund.

➤ **International stock or bond funds.** Foreign stock markets don't always perform like ours. International bond or stock funds can gain in value while Canadian funds perform poorly.

There are some funds that do the diversification for you. They are known as asset allocation funds (see Chapter 14).

Simple Mixes

Because each individual has different objectives, here are some suggested mixes of different kinds of mutual funds, based on your age and risk tolerance. (By the way, it's always a good idea to review your situation with an investment advisor, who can help you develop an appropriate asset mix).

Look Out!

Avoid investing in aggressive or speculative mutual funds if you can't handle sending the value of your investment on a roller coaster ride, or if you can't afford to lose.

➤ **Aggressive investors.** When you are young and just starting out or have built up a nest egg and still have a long time to invest before you retire, you can afford to invest aggressively. There is plenty of time for losses to be offset by gains in the share value of your mutual fund. That's why aggressive investors between the ages of 20 and 49 can invest 80 percent in stock funds and 20 percent in bond funds.

➤ **Moderate investors.** Investors between the ages of 50 and 59, who want to see the share value of their mutual fund or funds grow but want to protect their principal because they are nearing retirement, should invest 60 percent in stocks and 40 percent in bonds. Ages 50 through 59 are key savings and investing years when money is socked away for retirement a few years down the road. Because retirement is more than ten years away, growth in the value of the investments is important to building a retirement nest egg. This group should invest in stock funds for growth in the share value of their investments, but also needs to temper the risk of losing a lot of money.

➤ **Conservative investors.** Investors between the ages of 60 and 74 still need some growth so that the share value of their investments keeps pace with inflation. Then they can protect the purchasing power of their money. Consider a mix of 40 percent stocks, 40 percent bonds, and 20 percent money market funds.

➤ **Senior investors.** These investors, 75 and older, who need income but also need to preserve their principal, should keep 20 percent in stocks to help maintain the purchasing power of the money, 60 percent in bond funds, and 20 percent in money market funds. The biggest fear senior citizens face is outliving their money. That's why it's still important to keep a small percentage of investments in a well-managed stock fund.

Figure 7.3
Suggested Ways to Slice the Investment Pie (check with your investment advisor for the best mix for you).

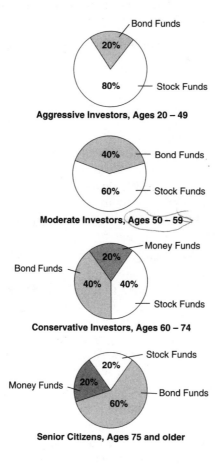

Aggressive Investors, Ages 20 – 49

Moderate Investors, Ages 50 – 59

Conservative Investors, Ages 60 – 74

Senior Citizens, Ages 75 and older

Spicing It Up

Want even more diversification? Invest in different kinds of stock and bond funds. A really aggressive investor can divide stock funds among aggressive growth funds (small company stock funds) or funds that invest overseas.

More moderate investors can split stock fund investments between dividend funds and international funds or keep a teeny-weeny bit in a well-diversified growth stock fund.

Conservative investors can invest in Canadian and U.S. dividend funds and short- or intermediate-term bond funds. A wide variety of bond funds are discussed in Chapters 12 and 13 of this book. It's always a good idea to mix and match your bond funds. If you need easy access to cash, you might want to have a money market fund. Long-term bond funds typically pay higher yields than short- or intermediate-term bond funds, but the short- and intermediate-term funds are less risky because their share value fluctuates less when interest rates change. For high yields, look at government mortgage bond funds, as well as corporate and international bond funds.

If you're really thoroughly diversified, you might have several kinds of funds. How much you invest in each type, as mentioned before, depends on your goals, how long you have to invest, and your risk tolerance.

Here are several types of funds you should consider when you want to diversify:

➤ A small company stock fund or aggressive stock fund

➤ A growth fund

➤ A dividend fund

➤ An international stock fund

➤ A corporate bond fund (also called a high-yield bond fund)

➤ An international bond fund

➤ A money market fund

Hot Tip

Most, if not all, of the major mutual fund companies have Web sites that you can access for information on their funds.

The Least You Need to Know

➤ Learn how much risk you can tolerate.

➤ Match the investment objectives of the funds with your tolerance for risk.

➤ Diversify your investments. By dividing up your investments among a variety of mutual funds that you are comfortable with, you can lower your overall risk—even though you may be investing in some riskier funds.

➤ Almost everyone should have some money invested in stock funds. Why? Stock fund share values grow more than the rate of inflation over the longer term.

Chapter 8

What Does All This Investment Stuff Cost?

In This Chapter

➤ Load, no-load—what's the difference?

➤ Other fees associated with mutual funds

➤ How to choose among mutual funds

You know now that there are hundreds and hundreds of mutual funds that cover a wide spectrum of areas: Canadian equity, international equity, bonds, money market, emerging growth companies, index funds etc. Now add one more selection to your plate: load and no-loads. As if you didn't have enough choices to make already!

I believe that you get what you pay for. In other words, identify your objectives first, then decide what type of fund you would like to invest in. Once you have identified the type of fund, you should look at *all* the funds in that category. There are many other things to consider when purchasing a mutual fund: performance, investment style, strength of the fund family, type of load, etc.

This chapter explains the main types of fees that mutual funds charge.

Loads, No Loads—What's the Difference?

Mutual funds are sold either as no-load funds or load funds. (Loads, commissions and sales charges all refer to the same fee.) When a mutual fund is sold *no-load* there is no charge to buy or sell the fund. Some no-load funds, however, may have set-up fee of approximately $45.

Load funds, on the other hand, have two options, *front-end load* and *back-end load*. Front-end load funds are sold with a charge that you pay when you buy the fund. The charge will range between 0 percent and 5 percent of the amount you are investing. The percentage is negotiated between you and your full-service broker or financial planner and typically falls in the range of one percent to three percent. (Discount brokers have a set rate they charge for front-end load funds that usually ranges from one percent to two percent.)

Technobabble

A *load* is the commission or sales charge associated with a mutual fund.

When you purchase a mutual fund with a front-end load you pay a charge or commission up front but pay nothing when you sell the fund. Therefore, you should consider purchasing a mutual fund with a front-end load when you have a time horizon of less than, say, five years.

On the other hand, when purchasing any load fund you have the option of purchasing it back-end load (alternately called rear-end load or a *deferred sales charge (DSC)*). When purchasing a fund with a back-end load, there is no charge when you purchase it however, there may be a charge when you sell it.

Here's how it works. When you purchase a back-end load fund, you pay no charge. However, depending on when you sell it, you will be charged a back-end load that applies on a declining scale basis. The charge for selling the fund is highest in the first year following the purchase and typically ranges from five percent to six percent in the first year and will decline each year until there is no charge at all for selling the fund. It will take anywhere from five to seven years on average for a back-end load to fall to zero. Time periods vary among fund families. Read your prospectus for complete details on the terms of the declining fee schedule.

Look Out!

Don't purchase a mutual fund simply because it is no-load. You should consider all information.

Usually, with funds that charge back-end loads, you are permitted to redeem up to 10 percent of the value of the fund each year without penalty. Also, most funds allow you to switch funds within the same family at no charge. So, if you intend to hold a fund for a while and you are investing in a solid family of funds, consider purchasing mutual funds with a back-end load. You can always switch to another fund within the family, if you wish.

Other Fees You Should Know About

MER

One of the key items to consider when purchasing a mutual fund—whether a load fund (front-end or back-end) or no-load—is the *MER (management expense ratio)*. It is what the mutual fund company charges the fund before any returns are paid out to the investor. The MER includes paying the manager to manage the fund and all other expenses associated with running the fund.

Although fund companies are regulated by law as to what can be charged to the MER, MERs tend to differ among fund companies. MERs are generally lower for money market and fixed-income funds and higher for equity funds. If the fund is invested outside of Canada it will tend to have a higher MER (MERs range from one percent for money market funds to more than two percent for high-maintenance funds like international equities.)

Keep in mind that the MER can differ between mutual funds in the same asset class (e.g., Canadian equity funds) or between different funds in the same family of funds. Make sure you know and compare MERs before you purchase a mutual fund.

Hot Tip

Most back-end funds allow you to redeem up to ten percent a year free of charge as well as switch to other funds in their family of funds free of charge.

Trailer Fees

All mutual funds pay trailer fees. Trailer fees are paid to your broker, financial planner, or discount broker. Trailer fees compensate your dealer on an ongoing basis to continually monitor the mutual fund for you. These fees are paid out *before* you receive your return and exist on every type of mutual fund, i.e., both load and no-load. The trailer fee will range from 0.0025% of assets invested in a money market mutual fund to 0.01% of assets in an equity fund. The trailer fee is not negotiable.

Hot Tip

A back-end load fund has a fee that is charged only on the sale of the fund. This fee is charged on a declining scale (to zero if held up to five to seven years in most cases).

Compare Costs Before You Invest

Use this handy checklist to zero in on the cost of potential funds.

Table 8.1 Compare Fund Fees

Fund Name	Load Percentage (if any)	Management Fee Percentage	Expense Ratio

Compare the fees for different funds before you choose one to buy.

At first glance it might seem advantageous to purchase all your funds no-load. Be careful though: there are many no-load funds that are good performers, but there are also many that are average or below-average performers. These ill-performing funds survive because they are able to attract clients by offering no charges to get into or out of the fund. The money you're saving with a no-load fund might very well be wiped out by lower-than-expected returns!

As you can see, mutual funds need to be fully researched before any purchases are made. The load is just one variable that should be considered when you purchase a mutual fund. Do your homework before you make any purchases. Mutual fund surveys and software packages can be enormously helpful. They'll do the analysis for you. You'll be able to compare loads, MERs, trailer fees, and much more!

The Least You Need to Know

➤ No-load mutual funds don't carry charges to buy or sell the fund; load funds can carry these charges, either up-front (hence the name front-end) or when you sell the fund (back-end).

➤ Be aware of the MER, trailer fee, and any other fees associated with purchasing the fund.

➤ Remember that while no-load funds don't charge you for buying or selling the fund, they aren't all great performers either. The money you're saving might be wiped out by lower-than-expected returns. Do your homework!

Chapter 9

Secrets of Mutual Fund Shopping

> ### In This Chapter
>
> ➤ How many mutual funds should you own?
>
> ➤ Deciphering important facts about how a fund invests
>
> ➤ Interpreting quarterly and annual fund reports
>
> ➤ Reading mutual fund tables in the newspapers

Do you routinely check the newspaper for sales on clothes and electronic gizmos? Smart shoppers do the same thing with mutual funds. Before you go to the shoe store for that year-end clearance sale, you first figure out how many pairs of shoes you need. Then you compare prices.

Picking a mutual fund works almost the same way. Before you shop, you have to figure out what types of mutual funds you want to own, how many to own, and how much you want to spend.

This chapter is a shopper's guide for mutual funds. You'll learn about the important documents you need to review before you invest in one or several mutual funds. Then, you'll discover a few quick ways to match a fund with your own personal needs.

How Many Funds Should You Own?

How many mutual funds should you own altogether? Just one? Or five or six?

One fund may not be enough. If you put all your money in one stock fund and the market tumbles, you could take a licking. That's why it's best to split the investment among at least two or three different kinds of funds.

Buy a baker's dozen and you have probably bought too many. Then you run the risk that the funds may own all or some of the same stocks. Not only that, but some of the stock fund managers could be buying the same stocks that your other mutual funds are selling. In fact, you actually could end up with the same investments that you started with, not to mention being overwhelmed with paperwork.

If you never have invested in anything other than bank accounts, it might be best to get your feet wet by first investing in a money market fund or by speaking with an investment advisor. After you've accumulated a few thousand dollars, you can take a big step toward building your wealth by investing in a balanced fund. Once you're comfortable with the growth and income that your balanced fund provides, you can begin splitting up the investment pie among a few types of funds.

The Magic Number

Five or six funds is a good number to have but, as you learned in Chapter 7, it's critical that you spread the investments among different types of funds. Your choices, depending on your investment comfort level and how long you intend to invest, probably should include the following:

➤ An aggressive growth or small company stock fund

➤ A growth fund

➤ A dividend fund

➤ An international stock fund

Sidelines

Don't want to go through the hassle of owning several funds? Yes, Virginia, it is possible to own just one fund that does all the work for you. *Asset-allocation funds,* which are a hybrid type of balanced fund, invest both in Canadian and foreign stocks and bonds. Some also invest in large or small company stocks. With asset-allocation funds, you invest in a wide variety of securities under one roof. Asset-allocation fund managers usually make slight adjustments in their funds' mix of investments, based on their professional evaluation of how the stock and bond markets will perform.

➤ A bond fund or income fund

➤ A short-term bond or money market fund

When you own a wide variety of funds, it's easy to change your investment mix as financial conditions shift. Recall that younger investors can start building their nest eggs with stock funds. As they get older and build up a hefty stash, they may want to preserve what they have by reducing their risk. Then they can put more into bond and money market funds and, when they retire, they'll start looking for funds to give them income and low risk.

Look Out!

It is important to review the prospectus carefully before you invest! Consult your investment advisor for a copy, or call the mutual fund company directly.

You also can split up your stock fund investments according to investment style. Chapter 4 discussed the difference between stock funds that invest for growth and funds that invest for value. It isn't a bad idea to own at least one fund that buys growth stocks and one fund that invests in undervalued stocks. These types of funds take turns outperforming each other, so if you own both of them, you have a better chance of having a winner.

Yuck! Read the Prospectus Before You Invest

Before you take one iota of your money and put it in a mutual fund, we sentence you to one of life's unpleasant little tasks—reading the fund's *prospectus*. Recall that this is the legal document that explains important information you need to know about the fund *before* you fork over your money. As a matter of fact, it is so important that a mutual fund company will send you one with your first purchase.

Don't worry. It's not quite as bad as it used to be—and we're here to help you along.

In the past, these things used to be in pure legalese. But now, fund companies typically send you a *simplified prospectus* that summarizes in plain English how to buy/sell their funds and their expenses and services along with detailed information on the individual mutual funds they offer. Many mutual fund companies have added charts and graphs, making it much easier for you to see at a glance how a fund has performed over time. Some issue warnings on the risks right up front. But keep in mind that these summaries are likely written, in part, by mutual fund companies' marketing departments, whose job is to get your business.

Technobabble

The prospectus is a legal document that tells important information about the fund, such as investment objectives, risks, fees, and who runs the fund. The *annual* and *quarterly reports* are fund updates that tell you what the fund did and how it performed for the period.

Figure 9.1   *The detailed fund description section of a simplified prospectus.*

UNIVERSAL CANADIAN GROWTH FUND

Fund Category	Date Started	Registered Plan Eligibility
Canadian Equity	*April 15, 1965* *Changed to Trust January 27, 1998*	*100% Eligible*

SUITABILITY

- the Fund is generally suitable as a core holding in a portfolio.

INVESTMENT OBJECTIVE

- primarily securities issued by Canadian corporations and government bodies to achieve long-term capital growth and provide a reasonable rate of return.

INVESTMENT STRATEGY

- generally fewer than 50 equity securities, in Canadian companies capable of delivering capital growth reliably over long periods.

- a disciplined stock selection process seeking companies with strong management, focused businesses, a 3 to 5 year investment horizon and a stock price which will generate acceptable returns.

FUND RISKS

- the Canadian stock and bond markets will usually have the greatest effect on the value of the Fund's equity securities.

- a significant decline in any one portfolio security could have a greater effect on the share price of the Fund than in a more diversified portfolio.

DISTRIBUTION POLICY

- the Fund's income is distributed annually, in December.

CALENDAR YEAR DISTRIBUTIONS

COMPONENTS	1993 $	1994 $	1995 $	1996 $	1997 $
Income	–	0.085	0.085	–	0.40
Capital Gains	0.13	0.152	0.152	–	0.85
Return of Capital	–	0.008	0.008	0.045	–
Total Annual Distributions	0.13	0.25	0.245	0.045	1.25

A meeting of investors of Universal Canadian Growth Fund Limited was held on December 2, 1997 to approve the conversion of the Fund from a corporation into a trust. Universal Canadian Growth Fund is the "new" Fund resulting from that conversion.

Source: Mackenzie Financial Corp.

To get the full picture, you need to cover all bases.

All prospectuses are required to present the same information to investors. It's a good idea to highlight or underline the most important information. Read the entire prospectus and pay close attention to the following sections, which may differ slightly from one prospectus to another:

Figure 9.2   *An example prospectus Table of Contents.*

TABLE *of* CONTENTS

Source: Trimark Mutual Funds.

Look at the investment objectives of the fund. In our illustration, it is labeled "Understanding our Investment Approach and Objectives." This tells how the fund intends to make money. It has a statement about the investment objectives and investment policy of the fund that you can match with your own investment objectives (see Chapter 7). Right off the bat you can tell the type of fund you are looking at. When you see words such as "maximum capital appreciation" or "capital growth," it's a sign that what you have in your hands is a prospectus for an aggressive growth fund. When you see "long-term growth," that's a sure sign the fund is a growth fund.

The fund expenses section explains the fees charged by the fund. In our illustration, it is labeled "Fees, Expense and Compensation Summaries." You'll learn how dealers are compensated for selling you the fund, and whether the fund has a load, or commission, or whether it's no-load, with no commission. As well, other fees and expenses charged to the fund are explained.

The sections about risks and investment restrictions tell how the fund could lose money and what investments the fund cannot make. In our illustration, it is listed as "Understanding Investment Risks."

It should explain whether the mutual fund uses risky investment tactics (by stating that the fund is "high-risk" or "aggressive") or borrows to invest in speculative stocks. You'll learn whether the fund is exposed to foreign currency risk or whether it invests in bonds issued by companies with poor credit ratings.

There also is information about the fund manager, the board of directors, and officers of the fund. In our illustration, it is listed as "Management Services."

The prospectus should offer information about how to buy and sell units. In our illustration, this is listed under two sections: "Buying Trimark Mutual Funds" and "Redeeming Trimark Mutual Funds." These sections tell how to set up an account with the fund and explain how to buy and sell units. There also will be information on automatic investment programs and switching funds within the fund family as well as withdrawal programs. Also covered is information on retirement savings plans such as RRSPs and RESPs. In our illustration, this section is listed as "Shareholder Services."

The distributions and tax information section tells you about the fund's tax implications. For example, depending on how the mutual fund company is set

Hot Tip

Examine the prospectus to determine whether the fund manager receives a bonus for doing a good job. Many investment companies reward a fund's portfolio manager for outperforming the market averages on similar funds. On the other hand, such a bonus could prompt the manager to take greater risks to show a more impressive return. More conservative investors should beware.

up, it may claim less taxable income. There is other information about taxes in this section, as well as important information stating the dates and frequency that distributions are paid to shareholders. In our illustration, it is listed as "Receiving Income and Capital Gains Distributions."

Read the Updates

Periodically, but at least once a year, you get progress reports on your fund, known respectively as quarterly and annual reports. You'll find out how the fund is doing and what stocks or bonds it owns. There are several important sections to the report:

➤ First, you get a message from the president of the fund recapping how the fund did in the past, including why the fund did or did not perform well, and the outlook for the future. For example, a stock fund's unit value might have increased because interest rates are low and corporate profits are high and expected to increase in the future. A bond fund's unit value might have declined because interest rates rose and the value of the fund's long-term bonds dropped. The last part of the section tells shareholders what the fund expects in the future. Sometimes the news is good and sometimes it's bad. A fund's president may say that the near-term prospect for stocks isn't rosy due to the prolonged recession. Over the longer term, however, as business conditions improve, the outlook for the fund's investments might improve.

➤ A comparison of how the fund performed versus its peer group's average and the market averages is also provided. Aha! There is usually a bar chart that shows you how the fund did versus the stock or bond market average over several time periods. You may also learn how the fund performed against an average of similar types of funds. A stock fund's financial report will list the percentage of the fund's assets invested in different industries, such as financial services, natural resources, leisure, and technology. That way you can see in which type of business your hard-earned money is invested.

➤ You also get a list of all the fund's investments and how much is in each security. Usually, there is a list of the top-ten holdings. You might write down the names of the stocks or bonds and look them up in other reports. You can learn about the companies, their revenues, expenses, profits, and business plans for the future. That way, you can get a feel for the types of investments a fund makes. If you see a fund that invests in Northern Telecom, Toronto Dominion Bank, BCE, Petro-Canada, etc., you know you are investing in blue-chip stocks. By contrast, if you see a list of names you don't necessarily recognize, you may be investing in small companies.

➤ If you invest in a dividend fund, balanced fund, or bond fund, there is information on how much dividend or interest income you received. If you invest in a small company stock fund or aggressive growth and growth funds, however, you may not see this information.

69

How to Check on Your Funds

You can check on your fund even more frequently. Simply check the daily mutual fund prices in your local newspaper's business section.

Every newspaper is a little different, but here's what most show:

➤ Each fund family is listed alphabetically, followed by the individual funds.

➤ Some tables do not list the investment objective of the fund; others do.

➤ The price or NAVPS (net asset value per share) that the fund closed at that day.

➤ Change means the number of cents the price of the fund went up or down, based on the previous day's closing price.

Table 9.1 Example of Mutual Fund Newspaper Quotations

Rainbow Mutual Funds	NAVPS*	Change
Rainbow Growth Fund	$17.85	+$0.10
Rainbow Balanced Fund	$15.52	+$0.02
Rainbow Bond Fund	$14.48	- $0.07

Net Asset Value Per Share or closing price as of last business day

Five Important Questions You Need to Answer

After you've looked at the prospectus and the mutual fund tables in your newspaper, be sure to check the following before you buy units:

1. Is this a fund that invests only in stocks? Or is it a lower-risk fund that invests in both stocks and bonds? Where does the fund invest? In Canada or outside Canada?

2. Is the investment style of the fund compatible with my objectives?

3. Do I want income from this fund? If so, what's the yield over the past several years?

4. Do I want to see my money grow over the years? If so, what's the fund's total return over at least the last five or ten years?

5. How many years has the portfolio manager been at the helm of the fund? What's his or her background?

The Least You Need to Know

➤ Read the fund's prospectus to learn the objective and risks of the fund before you invest.

➤ The prospectus' fee table shows how much the fund costs.

➤ It's generally best to own more than one or two funds, but no more than a dozen.

SECOND OPINION? FINE. YOUR INVESTMENT STINKS AND YOU'RE UGLY...

Chapter 10

Seeking a Second Opinion

In This Chapter

➤ Where to get a second opinion

➤ The best sources of information on funds

➤ The best newsletters for ongoing advice

You've picked up lots of information about mutual funds and, let's face it, you're no idiot. Why venture into totally unknown territory when the experts already have been there? It pays to see what the pros have to say about the mutual fund strategy you're considering.

This chapter takes a look at some important sources of mutual fund information that can help you pick funds and keep you up to date.

Check with the Experts

Although you feel close to being a mutual fund expert by now, it's always a good idea to get a second opinion, particularly if it's free. (At the library, you can find several excellent sources of information on mutual funds.)

The mutual fund reports, which we list in this chapter, all provide you with sufficient information to make a knowledgeable investment decision.

Mutual Fund Reporting Services

Most reports give you all the important ingredients you need to pick a fund. No matter what report you look at, you should get the following information:

- ➤ Past performance. This covers both total return and yield.

- ➤ Investment objectives.

- ➤ How funds rank in rate of return over fixed periods of time relative to other funds. Funds are ranked against all funds, as well as against funds with the same investment objective.

- ➤ Risk ratings.

- ➤ How much funds have made in total return when the market has gone up and how much they have lost when the market has gone down.

- ➤ Funds' fees, expenses, amounts needed to invest, addresses, and toll-free phone numbers.

Mutual Fund Information Resources

There are various resources you can tap when it comes to accessing the latest mutual fund information. Here's a list for starters:

- ➤ Business magazines. (e.g., *Maclean's*, *Report on Business*, *I.E. Money*)

- ➤ Mutual fund newsletters. (e.g., Gordon Pape's newsletters)

- ➤ Mutual Fund Web sites (The Fund Library, Globe Fund, individual fund companies' sites)

- ➤ Mutual Fund Tracking Software (e.g., BellCharts).

Look Out!

Not all mutual fund reporting services say the same things about the same funds. They all measure things a little differently. Look for a consensus of opinion from the reports or just stick with one report over the long haul rather than following one report for a month or so and then switching to another.

One of the best sources for mutual fund information is your home computer. As mentioned above, all of the major fund companies have their own Web sites chock full of information on their funds. As well, there are several independent sites that compile mutual fund information free for the taking. These include:

- ➤ The Fund Library at www.fundlibrary.com

- ➤ Globe Fund at www.globefund.com

Various software packages offer another avenue for mutual fund performance. One of the most user-friendly is BellCharts, which studies almost every mutual fund in Canada by comparing, sorting, and ranking funds by performance, type, size, volatility, and many more variables. BellCharts is updated on a monthly basis and a yearly subscription costs a few hundred dollars. Single issues are also available.

Find the Right Newsletter

Last, but not least, you have available to you a number of mutual fund newsletters. When selecting a newsletter, follow these tips on choosing one that's right for you:

➤ Request a free sample copy of the report before you subscribe.

➤ See whether the newsletter's investment philosophy is the same as yours. If you're a conservative investor, for example, you don't want to use a newsletter recommending a high-risk market-timing strategy.

➤ Determine whether the report includes news and information about the financial markets and the mutual fund industry.

➤ Make sure the newsletter gives advice on how to diversify based on your tolerance for risk, age, and investment goals.

➤ Compare the newsletter's returns versus the stock and bond market averages rather than relying on the newsletter's hype about its record.

➤ Consider a newsletter that has tracked mutual funds through at least one bull market and one bear market over the past three to five years.

➤ Subscribe only to a newsletter you can understand. Some are very technical and written for sophisticated traders. Others are written for the average investor.

➤ Call the newsletter before you subscribe. Find out whether the editor or investment advisor will answer any questions you may have during the year.

Hot Tip

You can call and get a free copy of most mutual fund newsletters. That way you can tell whether the report is right for you.

My Favourite Newsletters

To help you get started, here are a few newsletters I recommend:

➤ *The Canadian Mutual Fund Advisor.* Devoted exclusively to mutual funds, this advisory is published bi-weekly. New funds are spotlighted and existing funds are constantly monitored and reviewed for portfolio holdings, past performance, management style, and risk level. New subscribers receive a one-year introductory rate of $63.50. To subscribe, call MPL Communications collect at (416) 869-1177.

➤ The *Financial Post* publishes the quarterly *Survey of Mutual Funds*, which contains information on more than 1400 funds, a glossary of terms that defines fund types, year-over-year percentage changes in value, rates of return, and more. Each edition costs $69.95 and an annual subscription to four quarterly editions is $149.95. To order, call (800) 661-POST.

➤ *All-Canadian Mutual Fund Guide*. This guide delivers solid financial advice to create awareness about the possibilities within mutual funds. It's available at newsstands for $4.50 or you can call (416) 480-9425 to subscribe.

The Least You Need to Know

➤ It never hurts to see what the experts say about the mutual funds you're interested in.

➤ Remember that past performance is not indicative of future performance! Don't rely solely on return ratings. Look at the fund's history and the track record of the portfolio manager, as well as any other features offered by the fund and/or fund company.

➤ Get your friends to chip in with you for a subscription to a mutual fund news letter. You can use a newsletter as a source of information on the best funds to invest in, or you can use the newsletter to confirm your opinion of a fund you've already checked out.

Part 3
Zoning In on the Picks

This section of the book puts the different types of mutual funds under a microscope. You'll see exactly how money market mutual funds, bond mutual funds, and stock mutual funds stack up against each other and against similar investments. You'll learn how risky each type of fund is and get some idea of which funds might be right for you and which might not be.

Earlier chapters introduced you to the basics of mutual fund investing. The next chapters get into the nitty-gritty.

Chapter 11

Money Market Funds Versus Insured Bank Accounts

In This Chapter

➤ How do money market funds work?

➤ How to earn a higher return for your savings

➤ Other advantages of money market funds

Money market mutual funds are the closest thing to a bank account that you'll find in the mutual fund world. They are *not* CDIC-insured bank accounts, but often pay higher yields than similar bank accounts. This chapter examines exactly how risky money market funds are, whether they are for you, and the best ways to use them in your investment game plan.

Money Market Funds—The Least Risky

Whether you're starting out in the investment world, looking for a temporary parking place for some cash, or seeking to diversify your investment mix, money market funds are a low-risk starting place.

How can money market funds be so low-risk if they are not CDIC-insured?

As you learned in Chapter 3, money market funds invest in very short-term debt instruments. These debt obligations include Government of Canada Treasury Bills (T-bills) and commercial paper issued by corporations. When you loan money for such a short time to financially strong organizations, there's little risk your money fund won't be paid back.

Sidelines

Money market funds have been around for decades. The few such funds that were around in the '70s were an alternative for investors looking for low-risk ways to take advantage of high rates. By the early 1980s, when short-term interest rates hit double digits, even the most conservative investors began withdrawing money from GICs and putting money into money market funds. As of May 1998, money market assets totalled over $32 million, representing over 9 percent of the mutual fund industry's assets according to the Investment Funds Institute of Canada.

Even more importantly, money market mutual funds have one unique low-risk advantage over all other mutual funds. Whatever money you put into a fund, you should get back. Each share you buy is usually kept at a constant, often at $10. In effect, this means that exactly what you invest in a money market fund is exactly what you should get back. On top of that, a money market fund pays you interest income. You can take this interest in cash or plow it back into the fund and buy more shares.

Money market funds are subject to several investment rules aimed at preventing the portfolio managers from making risky investments, including the following:

➤ Recall from our discussion in Chapter 3 that long-term bonds can lose money when interest rates rise. You're unlikely to encounter this problem with money market funds. The average maturity of a money market fund should be 90 days.

➤ As with other mutual funds, a money market fund may invest no more than ten percent of its assets in any one company or government agency that raises money by issuing bonds. In fact, the maximum most funds invest in any one issuer is about two to three percent. This way, if one investment does happen to perform poorly, it should not dramatically affect the value of the entire fund.

➤ If a money market fund invests in corporate IOUs, also known as *commercial paper,* it's required that 95 percent of those corporate IOUs have the highest ratings by the Canadian Bond Rating Service or the Dominion Bond Rating Service.

Different Strokes for Different Folks

Assuming you can live without CDIC insurance, there are two types of money market mutual funds that you can buy either from a broker or directly from an investment company. The one you choose depends on your investment comfort level and tax situation:

➤ **Treasury bill funds.** These funds invest only in good old Treasury bills or T-bills, which are short-term IOUs of the Canadian Treasury. The funds typically pay the lowest yields, but are considered the least-risky investments. Treasury securities are backed against default by the "full faith and credit" of the Canadian government.

➤ **Money market funds.** These funds invest in:

➤ **Bankers Acceptances (BAs),** which are short-term loans to companies that export worldwide. Bankers Acceptances actually are secured by the goods that are to be sold.

Technobabble

Bankers' Acceptances are short-term loans used to finance exports. *Repurchase agreements* are collateralized overnight loans to banks. *Commercial Paper* are short-term loans to corporations.

➤ **Commercial Paper (CP),** which are short-term loans to large corporations.

➤ **Treasury bills,** which are short-term debt obligations issued by what most consider the most solid creditor of all: the Canadian Treasury. T-bills may be issued both federally and provincially.

➤ **Repurchase Agreements,** which are overnight loans to banks secured by Canadian Treasury Securities.

A Word About Bank Accounts...

Bank account yields are lower than those of most money market funds because bank accounts are CDIC-insured. Remember though, money market funds invest in T-bills that are backed by the federal government against default.

If you opt for CDIC insurance at a bank, remember that you are protected to only $60,000 per person.

Picking a Money Market Fund

Look at the type of investments the fund makes. The safest funds invest only in Canadian Treasury securities, but these funds may pay lower yields. The highest-yielding funds frequently invest in Commercial Paper.

Check the fund's expenses, listed in the prospectus as the expense ratio. The average money market fund has an expense ratio of 0.5 percent, but there are many lower than that.

Seek funds with wire-transfer capabilities. This enables you to move money electronically to and from your bank account and money market fund.

The Least You Need to Know

➤ Money market funds are the least-risky mutual funds.

➤ You can park money in a money market fund, then switch into other funds.

➤ Money market funds are not CDIC-insured.

➤ Money market funds typically pay higher yields than bank accounts and are considered a safe investment.

Chapter 12

Investing for Income: Bond Funds

In This Chapter

➤ Who should invest in a bond fund?

➤ How do bond funds differ from bonds?

➤ The unique risks of bond funds and how to reduce 'em

➤ Managing your bond funds when interest rates rise and bond prices fall

Why would anybody want or need a bond mutual fund? After all, you already learned about bonds in Chapter 3 and about the least-risky mutual funds, money market mutual funds, in Chapter 11.

What more could bond mutual funds possibly bring to the table? You'd be surprised. More than one-fifth of all mutual fund assets are in bond mutual funds or money market funds, according to the Investment Funds Institute of Canada's statistics for May 1998. Stock mutual funds carry more risk than money market or bond funds and don't generate interest income. Investors in bond funds get regular income with less risk than with stock funds.

In this chapter you'll learn whether you're better off buying a bond mutual fund or the bond itself. Although these guys both are in the same family, they are completely different animals. There are different risks and rewards to each. Read on, and you'll also learn some low-risk ways to make money from a bond mutual fund.

Who Should Have a Bond Mutual Fund?

Now we're getting into big-time investment. Invest in a bond fund, and you're investing in a riskier investment than a money market fund, in exchange for the longer-term potential of greater income and earnings. Before you even consider investing in a bond mutual fund—or any of the other mutual funds we're going to talk about in this chapter and beyond, for that matter—you must pull out some of the earlier pencil work you did. You need to re-examine the game plan you worked out in Chapter 2, listing your time horizons. Then, peek at the results of your risk-tolerance quiz in Chapter 6. Remember, you want money in a bond fund only if you can stomach seeing your original investment or principal fluctuate. Your bond mutual fund investment also should be just one facet of your long-range plan.

There are good reasons to invest in a bond mutual fund that could pay off handsomely down the road. First, you need to nail down whether these reasons fit your own personal needs and game plan. Then you need to figure out specifically how bond mutual funds fit the plan.

The great thing about bond mutual funds is they pay investors periodic interest income from the bonds in which they invest. To refresh your memory, bonds are loans to governments or corporations. The bond issuer, who is the borrower, agrees to pay the bondholder, or lender, interest on the loan and to repay the lender on a specific date.

Retirees Make Good Candidates

Bond mutual funds are particularly attractive for retirees or those who need regular income for living expenses. Bond mutual funds typically pay regular income, generally monthly or quarterly. With a bond mutual fund you can do the following:

➤ **Invest as little as $25 a month to get started.** Stand-alone bonds usually require a minimum initial investment of $5000.

➤ **Get professional management.** The portfolio manager selects and monitors the individual bond investments.

➤ **Become an owner of many investments.** You are well-diversified with a bond fund. It won't be the end of the world if one bond in the fund does poorly.

➤ **Switch funds or get cash with just a phone call.** If you need the cash, it's at your fingertips. Simply call your investment advisor or discount broker.

Do You Want to Diversify Your Investment Mix?

Bond funds are great for diversifying your investments. You don't want to put 100 percent of your money in the stock market if you can't tolerate the idea of losing a large chunk of your precious money. At least, that's the way we look at it! Because bond funds don't always move in the same direction as stock funds, a bond fund might perform well if a stock fund loses.

Bond Funds Versus Bonds

Although bond funds add a number of advantages to bonds themselves, there also are some major differences between these two investments. In fact, it pays to think twice before determining which you really want.

You might be pretty surprised to hear this, but an investment actually is *less risky* if it is invested directly in a Government of Canada bond and held to maturity than it is in a bond fund. With a bond, the Canadian government promises to pay your interest and to repay your principal at the end of the term. That's a guarantee from the nation's top creditor!

Yes, it's true that a bond fund might include Canadian government bonds. Nevertheless, you get no such principal guarantee with a mutual fund. Unlike bonds themselves, bond funds have no specific terms to maturity. Rather, these funds have an average maturity based on the maturity values of the bonds held (more on this in Chapter 13). The fund manager always is buying new bonds to replenish those that mature. As a result, the bond fund never matures.

We've been comparing Government of Canada bonds with Government of Canada bond funds. It works the same way with corporate bonds, however, as you will learn later in the chapter. Corporate bonds have an extra layer of risk compared to government bonds. Because you invest in a corporation, not the government, you run the risk that the corporation's business can sour and the company can have a tough time repaying the principal and/or paying interest on its bonds. This is why you will receive a higher rate of return for an investment in a corporate bond over a Government of Canada bond.

Recall from Chapter 3 that bond prices move in the opposite direction to interest rates. When interest rates rise, bonds prices fall. A bond fund investor who sells at the wrong time can take a licking.

Sidelines

Unlike a bond fund, a bond has a specific term to maturity and guarantees you'll get your principal back at the end of the term or when the bond is called. A bond fund carries no such guarantee because the fund manager always is buying and selling bonds. On the other hand, bond funds pay interest monthly or quarterly, but most bonds pay interest every six months.

Look Out!

As a general rule of thumb, the higher the yield on a bond fund, the greater the risk that you could lose money. You don't get something for nothing!

Bond Funds for Reliable Income

Bond funds are popular for two reasons: they pay periodic interest income to investors and many bond issuers guarantee the loan with collateral. Bond fund portfolio managers look for this collateral when they invest in bonds. This way, if the company issuing the bond goes under, a mutual fund likely gets at least something to resell and make back some of the losses.

Chapter 13 discusses the different kinds of bond funds and their investments in more detail.

Low-Risk Ways to Pad Your Pocket

Here are three strategies that potentially could boost your total return, while limiting some of the risk associated with bond funds:

1. If you are a low-risk-minded investor who is used to investing in GICs and money market funds, you may be able to earn more income by investing in *short-term bond funds*, which you learned a little about in Chapter 4, but will explore further in Chapter 13. These funds have longer average maturities than money market funds. Don't forget, though, by extending your maturity, you are taking on a bit more risk.

2. Bond fund investors can make more money with little more risk by investing in Canadian government bond funds, rather than funds that invest directly in Canadian Treasury bonds. Government bonds, like Treasury bonds, are backed by the "full faith and credit" of the Canadian government against default, but have maturities of one year or more.

3. Invest in corporate bond funds because they will pay you a higher return (for taking on more risk compared to Government bonds). Of course, your total return can vary based on interest rates and business conditions.

Hot Tip

If the bonds in your bond fund are issued by the Canadian Treasury or government, don't worry too much about those agencies going under. You still could lose big, though, if interest rates rise or inflation escalates.

Unique Risks and How to Reduce 'Em!

Unfortunately, there's no free lunch when you invest in bond funds.

Before you invest in a bond fund, it is important to do your homework so that you don't get burned by this investment. Here's what to watch for:

➤ A company that issues a bond to your mutual fund could default on its interest and principal payments.

Solution: Stick with bond funds that invest only in the strongest companies and governments. Fortunately, two major companies, Canadian Bond Rating Service and Dominion Bond Rating Service rate bond issuers' strength. The types of bonds and their ratings will be spelled out in the fund prospectus or ask your investment advisor.

➤ Bonds rated AAA are the least risky. As illustrated in Table 12.1, there are different rating classifications. As you go down in ratings, you will receive more in interest to compensate you for taking on the additional risk.

➤ As you learned in Chapter 3, when interest rates rise, bond prices fall. Unfortunately, many investors learned this the hard way in 1994. The longer the maturity of the bond, the greater the risk of a price decline. (Chapter 13 shows how much the price of your bond fund changes when interest rates change.)

Solution: Limit your losses by investing in short- or intermediate-term bond funds. The longer the term, the greater the risk.

➤ The steady income from your bond fund may not be enough down the road to cover the rising prices of groceries, gas, utilities, and clothes. This is known as inflation.

Solution: Invest regularly in your bond fund. You buy more units when bond rates are higher, so you get more income over the years.

Table 12.1 Bond Credit Ratings

Dominion	Canadian	Meaning
AAA	A++	Highest quality bonds. Unquestioned credit quality.
AA	A+	Very Good quality, but slightly more risk than triple-A-bond issuers.
A	A	Good quality or Upper Medium, but issuers don't have the financial strength of triple or double-A-rated issuers.
BBB	B++	Medium-grade bonds. Short-term financial strength of issuer is good, but there could be long-term risks.
BB	B+	Lower Medium Grade.
B	B	Poor Quality.
CCC	C	Speculative Grade
CC	D	In Default
C	Suspended	Lowest Standing

What to Do When Interest Rates Rise

It was rapidly rising interest rates that caused many bond fund investors to lose five to eight percent in 1994. Does that mean that the next time interest rates shoot up, you should sell?

Nope, with a capital N. There are several ways to cut losses on your bond fund. You may have to do some fund switching to protect yourself, but it's not all that complicated. Here are just a few ideas:

1. **Just calmly sit tight and reinvest bond fund distributions.** Interest rates go up and down all the time. Even if interest rates rise over the shorter term and a long-term bond's price has dropped, investors should profit over time.

2. **Invest in a money market fund to play it safe.** Then every month, take money out of the money market fund and put it into an intermediate-or long-term bond fund. You'll earn higher yields, but you don't have to worry about losing a bundle as if you had invested a big chunk of money in a bond fund. For very conservative investors, for example, take out 50 percent.

3. **Diversify your fixed-income investments.** We've already warned you about this. Don't put all your eggs in one basket. Invest in different types of fixed-income investments, maybe a couple of types of bond mutual funds as well as a couple of bonds. Even though corporate bonds are riskier than government bonds, you might want to think about investing a small percentage into a corporate bond fund to complement your government bonds and earn a higher rate of return.

4. **Ladder your bond funds.** Don't invest in only one bond fund. Put money in bond funds that have different average maturities. Invest in a money market fund, short-term bond fund, intermediate-term bond fund, and a long-term bond fund. You'll earn high yields, but with less risk than putting all your money in one long-term bond fund. Chapter 13 discusses the average maturity of bonds owned by short-term, intermediate-term, and long-term bond funds.

The Least You Need to Know

➤ Invest in bond funds for steady income.

➤ Bond funds pay monthly or quarterly income; individual bonds typically pay interest income every six months.

➤ In most cases, fixed-income products like government and corporate bond funds are more risky than money market funds, but they're safer than equity or stock investments.

➤ Make regular investments in a bond fund to combat inflation. When inflation rises, interest rates rise. By investing regularly, you can earn higher yields to keep pace with inflation.

➤ One of the keys to a successful portfolio is diversification. Therefore, you should probably have some exposure to fixed-income investments in your portfolio.

Finding the Right Kind of Bond Funds

In This Chapter

➤ Types of bond funds

➤ Picking a bond fund that's right for you

➤ Avoiding the biggest mistakes with bond funds

You now know that bond mutual funds are great for providing regular monthly or quarterly income, they're convenient, and they're less risky than many stock mutual funds, so it may be a good idea to have one in your hip pocket.

In this chapter, you'll learn how to tell a good bond mutual fund from a bad one and exactly how to stay clear of the high-risk bond funds. You'll see how much of an impact rising rates can have on the value of your investment, and you'll find out what to ask to make sure you're getting the best deal you possibly can.

How Long Is Your Bond Fund?

Here's the long and short of investing in bond funds, so to speak. As you learned in Chapter 4, there are bond funds that invest for the short, intermediate, and long term in Canadian government bonds or notes, corporate bonds, and, occasionally, foreign securities. In general, the higher-yielding bond funds in each category—in other words, the funds that pay the most—typically invest a larger percentage of their assets in corporate and/or foreign bonds and notes. The lower-yielding funds in each category generally invest more heavily in Canadian Treasury or government agency bonds or notes. You learn more about these different categories of bond funds later in this chapter.

It's important to understand how the average maturity of your bond fund can affect your total return.

Short-Term Funds

Short-term bond funds generally own a portfolio of bonds with an average maturity of three years. This doesn't mean they invest *only* in bonds with those terms. They can own some bonds that mature in five, ten, or twenty years or they can invest in cash or money market instruments that mature in 90 days or less and notes that mature in three to five years. Add everything up, though, and the average maturity of a short-term bond fund is about three years.

Short-term bond funds generally provide a less-risky bond fund investment—one that will not show large increases or declines in total return. Although they generally pay higher yields than GICs or money market funds, the total return of short-term bond funds is less vulnerable to changes in interest rates than funds that invest in longer-term bonds. That makes them a good short-term parking place for your money. Remember, if interest rates rise one percent, a $1000 investment in a short-term bond fund drops three to four percent.

Intermediate-Term Funds

The average bond owned by an intermediate-term bond fund matures in five to ten years. The total return, however, is more volatile on intermediate-term bond funds than it is on short-term bond funds. If interest rates rise or fall one percent, the total return of an intermediate-term bond fund falls or rises about six respectively.

Look Out!

Don't forget our previous warning that you can lose money even with the least-risky bond funds if interest rates rise. That's why it's critical that you avoid putting all your money in investments with the same maturity.

Intermediate-term bond funds are ideal investments for individuals with a moderate tolerance for risk. Typically, you receive about 85 percent of the interest income that you would receive from long-term bond funds; however, intermediate-term bond funds have less-volatile total returns. That makes intermediate-term bond funds a good long-term investment for those who want income or modest growth in the value of their investment over the longer term. They can be used as a lower-risk way to save for a child's college education, a downpayment on a house, or retirement.

Long-Term Funds

Long-term bond funds invest in bonds with an average maturity of 10 to 20 years. Long-term bond funds tend to pay the highest interest rates, but their total returns are more volatile. The total return on long-term bond funds can be -12 percent or +12 percent when interest rates rise or fall one percent respectively. As a result, long-term bond funds are best suited for investors with a high tolerance for risk. The bond funds can be used as a source of retirement income, for a long-term savings plan, or to help you diversify your investments.

Narrowing the Field

Don't worry, troops. Choosing a bond fund is not an impossible task. In fact, it's kind of like buying detergent, which we all manage to do on a regular basis, right? There are detergents for cold water and detergents for hot water. You use some for towels and sheets, and others are for delicate fabrics. Wash your underwear with the wrong kind of detergent, and you wind up scratching yourself all day.

Fortunately, we've already given you the basics to avoid scratching yourself with bond funds. You already know these facts:

➤ Bond funds issued by the Canadian Treasury or government agencies are the least risky. You have the backing of the Canadian government against default.

➤ There are two agencies that rate the credit risk associated with bonds: the Dominion Bond Rating Service (DBRS) and the Canadian Bond Rating Service (CBRS).

➤ The longer the average maturity of the bonds in your fund, the greater the risk. For lower risk, invest in short-term or intermediate-term bond funds.

➤ Invest regularly in your bond fund to combat inflation. Then, when inflation heats up and bond rates rise, you can invest to take advantage of the situation.

Your Best Bets

It's time to narrow down your choices. If low risk is important to you, I suggest you look at your fund's investment objective. Below are the different types of bond funds listed from safest to most aggressive.

Canadian Treasury Bond Funds (T-Bill Funds)

Treasury bond funds invest in Canadian Treasury bonds and notes. T-bills are backed by the Canadian federal government and are very liquid, meaning you can sell them on the open market at any time prior to maturity. They have maturities of one year or less and are a great place to park your money for the short-term.

Money Market Funds

Money Market Funds include T-bills as well as Commercial Paper and Bankers' Acceptances. They offer higher yields than T-bill funds and are safe, liquid investments.

Mortgage Funds

Mortgage-Backed Security (MBS) funds are issued by the Canada Housing and Mortgage Corporation (CMHC), an agency of the federal government. Consequently, the Canadian government guarantees the MBS. If interest rates rise, you can still lose money, but remember, as always, the shorter the average term to maturity the less risky the fund.

Canadian Government Bond Funds

Government bond funds include not only the Government of Canada, but also provincial and municipal bonds. Keep in mind that each government bond issue will be rated. Be sure that you understand the different bond ratings.

High-Yield Bond Funds

These funds have become more popular recently because they offer higher yields than Government of Canada bonds especially in a lower-interest-rate environment. Before you invest in this type of fund, be sure you understand what the fund is allowed to invest in. The prospectus will spell out the investments as well as the lowest-rated debt instruments that the fund can invest in. These funds will usually have a mix of government bonds with corporate bonds. As you are assuming more risk by investing in high-yield bond funds, you are compensated with a higher return, hence the name "high yield."

Technobabble

High-yield bond funds invest in bonds issued by corporations. You'll earn higher rates of return on these bond funds for taking on additional risk. Remember—unlike government bonds, corporate bonds are not guaranteed against default.

International Bond Funds for Diversification

There are all types of international bond funds, with varying degrees of risk. Once you get into international bond funds, however, you are adding one extra element of risk to the whole mutual fund bond proposition. Fund managers must convert Canadian dollars into foreign currency to buy the bonds. Therefore, if the value of the Canadian dollar rises against foreign currencies, the value of your investment can drop. True, you can earn higher yields and make bigger profits in funds that invest in some international bonds, but they're not for beginners. Nor do you want to sock all your money in them.

Given that caveat, the international bond funds considered least risky invest in bonds issued by foreign governments worldwide. Others invest in governments and large multinational corporate bonds. All these types of mutual funds are among the least risky of the international bond funds. The fund managers diversify not only by country but also by corporate bond issuers and the industries of the companies.

There also are bond funds that invest in Latin American bonds and other emerging markets. These are high-risk investments because these countries may be politically or economically unstable.

As in this country, you can tell a well-managed international bond fund by looking at things like total return as well as yield. You don't want to invest in a high-yielding international fund only to find the market value of your investment declining. Investors want to see that the fund is managing its investments properly. That means international bond fund managers try to limit losses when interest rates rise and bond prices fall. If they believe interest rates are rising in one country, they may invest in another where rates are expected to decline. They may reduce the average maturity of the fund to cushion the blow of rising interest rates in some countries.

The world's economies don't move the same way our bond markets do. There's a good chance that when rates are low in Canada, they are higher elsewhere. That's why a well-diversified international bond fund that invests in government and/or high-quality corporate bonds can be a good deal. You might consider keeping a small part of your bond fund holdings in a well-managed bond fund that invests worldwide. Remember, though—when you invest in international bonds, you face an extra layer of risk, because of your exposure to the fluctuation of the currency exchange rate. That's why it's a good idea to keep only a small part of your bond fund holdings in these types of funds.

The Long and Short of It

See? That wasn't so bad, was it? You've figured out which type of bond fund you want to invest in based on the amount of risk you can tolerate. The next step is to determine the average maturity of the bonds you want in your fund. Should you invest in a short-, intermediate-, or long-term bond fund?

As we told you in earlier chapters, you earn higher yields with longer-term bond funds. Of course, there's a trade-off. When interest rates rise, longer-term bond funds drop more in value.

Hot Tip

Better idea: hedge your bets by dividing your investments among short-, intermediate- and long-term bond funds.

95

Here is how the value of a $1000 investment changes if interest rates change one percent. As you can see, if interest rates rise one percent, the value of your $1000 investment in a short-term fund drops only $25—but a long-term bond fund drops 68 smack-a-roos:

Table 13.1 Bond Fund Returns and Interest Rate Changes

Type Rates	Rise 1%	Fall 1%
Short-term	$975	$1025
Intermediate-term	953	1047
Long-term	932	1068

As a rule, short-term bond funds are less risky than longer-term bond funds. Follow these rules:

➤ Invest in a short-term bond fund if you are investing for two years or less.

➤ Invest intermediate-term if you are investing for more than two years, or if you want to play it safe with your principal and still get decent income from your fund over your lifetime.

➤ Invest in long-term bond funds if you want higher income and you can tolerate seeing the value of your principal drop ten percent or more in any given year.

Avoid These Mistakes

There's a lot of material to digest when considering a bond mutual fund. If you decide to go that route, try not to make the following costly errors. You'll save a lot of heartache—*and* money by not:

➤ Chasing after high-yield funds without understanding the risks.

➤ Investing in long-term bond funds when you only want to park your money for less than a year.

➤ Paying high management expense ratios for your bond fund. Be sure to check the prospectus.

➤ Forgetting to consider the currency exchange issue when investing in foreign bond funds.

How to Pick a Bond Fund

You have to do your homework when you invest in bond funds:

➤ Read the bond fund's prospectus before you invest to be sure the fund's investment objectives match your own.

➤ Ask yourself why you want to invest in this fund. Do you need the interest in-come to live on? Do you want to diversify your investments—hedge your stock fund investments by owning a bond fund? Or do you want to use a bond fund as a temporary place to park your money until an investment comes along?

➤ How long do you expect to invest?

➤ Decide whether you want to invest in short-, intermediate- or long-term bond funds.

➤ Compare similar bond funds' charges. Use the Bond Fund Selection Worksheet to help out:

> ➤ What is the management fee?

> ➤ What's the expense ratio, or percentage of assets taken out to cover expenses?

> ➤ What does the fund yield compared with other funds? You can check various bond fund reports like the one on page 93 to compare.

> ➤ Look at the fund's total return over at least three years. You don't want to own a high-yielding fund only to discover the total value of your invest-ment is declining. You want consistent returns, not wild price swings.

> ➤ Check the credit ratings of the fund's holdings, which are listed in the fund's prospectus and quarterly reports.

Table 13.2 Top 10 Bond Funds

Ten Years	% Return
1) Altamira Bond	12.7
2) SSQ—Obligations Canadiennes	12.0
3) Altamira Income	11.8
4) McLean Budden Pool Fixed Income	11.8
5) Desjardins—Laurentian Bond	11.6
6) Batirente—Sec Obligations	11.4
7) Montrusco Select Income	11.4
8) PH&N Bond	11.4
9) Equitable Life Seg Accum	11.1
10) Optimum Obligations	10.9

Average Annual Return 10 Years Ended May 1998.
Source: BellCharts

Table 13.3 Bond Fund Selection Worksheet

Fund	Yield	Load	Management Fee	Expense Ratio	Terms—S,I,L

Use this worksheet to compare different bond funds.

The Least You Need to Know

➤ For safety, invest in a T-bill or money market fund.

➤ Short-term bond funds lose less money when interest rates rise than longer-term bond funds.

➤ Longer-term bond funds pay higher yields.

Chapter 14

Building Your Wealth with Stock Funds

In This Chapter

➤ Why do stock funds grow in value?

➤ The different types of stock funds

➤ Building your wealth for the long term

With this chapter, you're headed into the big stakes. Of all the major types of mutual fund investments, stock mutual funds can make you the most money fastest. They also can lose the most equally as fast.

This chapter discusses how stock mutual funds work. You'll learn about each category of stock fund and how it is best used. Stock mutual funds, we admit, are not for the faint-hearted. When used as part of a long-term diversified plan, however, they can provide a significant hedge against inflation and play a key role in building your wealth.

Stock Funds Are Long-Term Affairs

Buy a stock mutual fund for as little as $25 a month inside a monthly purchase plan and—congratulations—you're the owner of not one, but many businesses!

Of course, you need a certain mentality to own a business, and it's a good idea to refer to your risk-tolerance quiz in Chapter 6 to see exactly how much of that stuff you have. With a stock mutual fund, you need to be prepared to take the lumps as well as the good times that come not only with your fund's stocks themselves, but also with the economy and the stock market. Fortunately, the fact that you own not one, but several, businesses in a mutual fund, and for such a potentially small up-front investment, helps make the whole idea of stock mutual funds palatable for many investors.

To get an idea of how a stock mutual fund can quietly build wealth, let's peek in on Comfortably Retired Ralph. When Ralph was in his early 30s in 1959, he started investing in a stock mutual fund. He decided to invest $100 a month in a blue-chip common stock fund. Ralph had been dabbling in stocks for several years at the time, so he knew how stocks worked. This time, Ralph was looking for something he could buy and hold until he retired. He settled on the Rainbow Growth Fund.

Everything went well until 1961. The Rainbow Growth Fund was up almost 30 percent over the first two years. Then wham! The economy turned sour. The economy went into a recession and the Rainbow Growth Fund lost 14 percent. Ralph's wife, Eleanore, wanted him to sell, but Ralph refused. He was stubborn.

Fortunately, the Rainbow Growth Fund had some smooth sailing after that. The fund made back its losses and more. The total return on the fund was 19 percent in the fourth year. Then boom! In 1973 and 1974, the value of Ralph's stash plummeted 45 percent. Those were bad years for the economy and the stock market.

Did Ralph sell? No. He hung in there, although it was an incredibly tough decision. Eleanore even threatened to get a divorce at one point. Ralph just kept pumping $100 a month into his stock fund. The move turned out to be a good one. By the time Ralph retired at age 66 in 1994, his $100-a-month mutual fund investment was worth $481,000. His investment grew at an annual average total return of 11.8 percent.

Now, Comfortably Retired Ralph always has a smile on his face. He and Eleanore retired to Boca Raton, Florida several years ago. They have their pension, other income, and a nice mutual fund nest egg. The investment continues to grow.

Ralph did pretty darned good.

Of course, past performance is no indication of future results. Nevertheless, this gives you an idea of how a stock fund can do if you invest for the long term. Invest in a stock fund for the short haul, however, and you can lose a lot.

Is the Risk of Losing Money Worth the Return?

Ralph kept his Rainbow Growth Fund through the rough periods. Whenever the stock market loses more than ten percent, it's sometimes referred to as a *bear market*. There have been a number of bear markets over the years, but, so far, the stock market has bounced back after about a year. Then *bull markets* occur when the stock market moves higher for a couple of years running.

Ralph could have bailed out in 1973 or 1974 during the worst bear market since the Great Depression. Many of his friends did. They sold and took their losses. In fact, some swore off mutual funds forever. However, those with the courage to stay put made their losses back and more. Over the past ten years, the Toronto Stock Exchange 300 Index, which comprises 300 widely traded Canadian stocks, has returned a 11 percent average annual return.

How Stocks Grow

Stock funds tend to outperform other investments in the long term largely because ownership in corporations is one of the best ways to make money. During periods of economic prosperity, business profits. As a result, owners of the companies profit.

The ABC Pen Company, for example, is having a great year. It can sell its pens for $2 each instead of the $1.59 it charged last year. Meanwhile, it costs no more to produce and sell the pen. The owners of the company are happy because the stock they bought at $10 a share now sells for $14 a share. That's how both stocks and stock mutual funds grow in value.

Over the long term, stocks have outperformed all other types of investments, such as bonds and GICs. Of course, just as Comfortably Retired Ralph experienced, there have been dips along the way. That happens during an economic recession. Businesses start to lose money and people get laid off.

Remember, you never can predict the future when it comes to mutual fund investing. However, history *does* give you at least some idea of what you can expect from a well-managed stock fund over the long term.

Is the risk worth the return? It sure is if you have a game plan, know why you are investing, and do it for a long time. Chapters 6 and 7 helped you zero in on your tolerance for risk, then helped you match up your investment comfort level with the right funds. There are different kinds of stock funds— some more risky than others. If you are not prepared to invest for an absolute minimum of three to five years—you should stick with less-risky money market funds and short-term bond funds.

Sidelines

Stock funds are one of the best ways to protect your money from the ravages of inflation. The price of goods and services rose at about 2.5 percent annually over the past decade. Stock funds, on average, grew at an annual average total return of 11 percent. Therefore, less 2.5 percent inflation a year, stock funds grew at an annual average total return of 8.5 percent. You were more than protected from rising prices.

Look Out!

Stock mutual funds are the riskiest type of mutual fund. To minimize losses, anyone considering stock mutual funds should be prepared to keep the investment a rock-bottom minimum of three to five years.

Sidelines

What do stock fund portfolio managers look for in a company before they invest? Of course, no two fund managers think alike. However, they make their decisions based on a number of factors:

- Most professional fund managers visit or talk to a company's management to discuss the firm's business plans and goals. The manager wants to know what the company has up its sleeve in regard to research, development, and marketing, as well as how financial problems are being solved.

- Fund managers look at a company's financial statement for gems of information about financial strength and profitability. They may want to own companies whose profits have been rising over the past couple of years, or may spot stocks selling at very low prices in relation to their future earnings potential.

- Fund managers may look at a company's industry to evaluate how it will do in the future. For example, when the economy is picking up steam, employment is high and people spend money. Then leisure, entertainment, and airline stocks do well. People tend to buy houses when interest rates decline. Then homebuilding stocks do well. By contrast, when a recession is looming on the horizon, businesses serving basic necessities, such as utilities and food manufacturers, tend to do well.

- Some fund managers look at trends. They buy stocks that are showing strong upward price trends. They sell based on downward price trends.

If You're an Aggressive Investor...

Although stock funds in general are riskier than bond funds and money market funds, there are different categories of stock funds, and some are riskier than others. You can curb your risk a bit based on the type of stock fund you select. Keep in mind that the more conservative your fund, the fewer price swings you'll have—and those price swings can be up as well as down. The next sections present the most aggressive categories of stock funds, which can bring you the greatest returns as well as the greatest losses.

Aggressive Stock Funds or Small Company Stock Funds

Recall from Chapter 4 that aggressive stock funds, or small cap (also called small company funds) invest in mostly small companies. Small cap funds own little acorns that can grow into oak trees. The funds buy new companies or smaller companies that plow all their profits back into their businesses. These companies may have annual revenues in the millions of dollars a year. By contrast, blue-chip companies pull in several billion dollars in revenue per year. Most small cap fund managers use the growth-stock investment style. They invest in rapidly growing companies whose earnings also are growing rapidly. Many of these companies, but not all, are in the technology business.

There also are small cap funds that look for undervalued stocks—overlooked companies that should register strong profits in the future. The fund managers buy and hold stocks for the longer term. These fund managers look for gems. They buy early and wait for the companies to do well. Then they profit when others invest.

You can go for a wild ride when you invest in a small cap fund. Small cap stocks perform in streaks. They may do well for three or four years running. Then they die before things pick up again. That's why you have to invest in them for the longer term. The average small cap fund gained 10.6 percent over the past decade (Source: BellCharts).

Table 14.1 Top-Performing Small Company Stock Funds, Average Annual Total Return, 10 Years Ending May 1998

Fund	Average Annual Total Return %
Marathon Equity	20.8
Mawer New Canada	15.8
Sceptre Equity Growth	15.5
Quebec Growth Fund Inc.	15.1
Altamira Special Growth	14.7
Spectrum United Canadian Growth	12.7
General Trust of Canada Growth	12.5
Multiple Opportunities	12.0
Guardian Enterprise Classic	11.8
Saxon Small Cap	11.3

Source: *BellCharts*, May 1998

Growth Funds

Growth stock funds are typically a little different than aggressive growth or small company stock funds. Growth funds stick with proven companies that have a solid track record of sales and profits. These funds invest in mid-sized and larger well-established, well-managed companies—brand-name companies.

Sidelines

How do you pick a stock fund? When shopping for a stock fund, look for the following:

- Compare a fund's year-by-year performance. Avoid funds with wide swings in annual returns (large swings are to be expected with small cap funds). Invest in funds with the most consistent year-by-year returns.

- Compare a fund's annual average returns over at least a three-to-five-year period.

- Compare how the fund did in bad years such as 1981, 1984, 1987, 1990, and 1994. You want the fund that lost the least amount of money.

- Check the fund's prospectus and annual report to be sure the investment objective of the fund is in line with the type of stocks it owns.

- Check the fund's prospectus for the fund's expense ratio and loads. You want the fund with reasonable expenses and the best track record so that you will earn more money.

Talk to your investment advisor or financial planner to get a professional opinion.

Some growth funds like to buy and hold undervalued stock for a few years. These funds are characterized by low portfolio turnover, so you are likely to see some of the same stocks in your growth fund's portfolio for a couple of years running. By contrast, other growth funds turn over the stocks they own more than once a year. These funds look for rapid profits from the sale of securities. Because these funds have a higher turnover, you are likely to receive annual capital gains distributions, which result when the fund sells a stock for profit during the year.

As a group, Canadian growth funds have delivered an average 10-year return of 10.9 percent (Source: BellCharts).

Index Investing

The performance of the markets is measured by an index. Each index comprises a basket of stocks or bonds. While you can use an index as a benchmark to gauge how your mutual funds are doing by comparing one to the other, you can also buy index mutual funds. Index mutual funds mirror a given market index. While there are dozens of market indices worldwide, the most widely used ones include:

Table 14.2 Top-Performing Growth Funds, Average Annual Total Return, 10 Years Ending May 1998

Fund	Average Annual Total Return %
AIC Advantage	23.5
Altamira Equity	20.3
Montrusco Select Growth	18.3
Phillips Hager and North Vintage	17.5
Bissett Canadian Equity	16.0
McLean Budden Pooled Cdn. Equity Growth	14.5
Dynamic Canadian Growth	14.4
Westbury Canadian Life "A"	14.0
Spectrum United Cdn. Equity	13.3
AGF Growth Equity	13.1

Source: *BellCharts*, May 1998

The TSE 300: This index tracks 300 Canadian stocks that trade on the Toronto Stock Exchange, which include some of Canada's largest companies like BCE, Canadian Pacific, and Seagram.

The Dow Jones Industrial Average (DJIA): This index tracks the movement of 30 of the largest blue-chip stocks in the United States that trade on the New York Stock Exchange, such as Coca-Cola™, IBM and AT&T.

The S&P 500 (Standard & Poor 500): This index tracks 500 blue-chip stocks in the United States. It's the benchmark to which most U.S. portfolio managers compare themselves. No small stocks are included.

The EAFE Index: This is the Morgan Stanley Capital International Europe, Australia, and Far East Index. If you want to track more than 1000 foreign stocks in 20-odd countries, check this one out. It's considered the most prominent index for investing in foreign countries.

You should be able to find mutual funds that mirror the above-mentioned indices. Buying an index fund is a great way to buy into hundreds of the largest, most-profitable companies in the world. And you can do this with as little as $25 a month! For long-term growth and diversification, consider these funds. Do keep in mind that these funds move with the corresponding market—so as the market goes up, the fund should as well, and vice versa. To get a better handle on market indices, follow them in the business section of the newspaper, or on your local TV news.

More Conservative Wealth-Building Funds

Some funds are designed for more conservative investors. These investors are willing to risk their principal a little in exchange for greater long-term profits, but can't bear the thought of large losses in their portfolios. The next sections discuss these funds.

Dividend Funds

Dividend funds are great investments for moderate investors. (Refer to your risk-tolerance quiz in Chapter 6.) The objective of this type of fund is long-term growth of your money, plus income. Dividend funds can achieve this goal because they invest in blue-chip stocks. When you have blue-chip stocks, you are an owner of Canadian companies that have stood the test of time. Sure, they may lose some money when there's a recession, but their profits keep rising almost every year.

The secret of dividend fund investing is reinvesting the income your fund gets from these blue-chip companies such as Toronto Dominion Bank, BCE, Petro-Canada, Seagram, etc. If these businesses continue to grow and profit, so will your investment in them through your dividend fund.

You don't get as big a bang for your buck from dividend as you would from more aggressive stock funds, but you get a steadier investment. The income from the fund cushions some of the losses when the value of the fund declines. As a group, dividend funds returned an average 11.3 percent over the past ten years.

Hot Tip

Dividend funds are good investment choices for those who want reduced risk from straight growth funds and a steady level of income.

Table 14.3 Top-Performing Dividend Funds, Average Annual Total Return, 10 Years Ending May 1998

Fund	Average Annual Total Return %
Phillips Hager & North Dividend Income	16.5
AGF Dividend	13.9
Greenline Dividend	13.7
Maxxum Dividend	13.4
Scotia Excelsior Dividend	12.3
Bissett Dividend Income	12.0
Investors Dividend	11.9
Industrial Dividend Growth	10.8
BPI Dividend Income	10.7
Strategic Value Dividend	10.6

Source: *BellCharts*, May 1998

Table 14.4 Top-Performing Balanced Funds, Average Annual Total Return, 10 Years Ending May 1998

Fund	Average Annual Total Return %
ABC Fully Managed	16.4
FMOQ Investment	15.7
McLean Budden Balanced Growth	13.2
Ferique Balanced	12.7
FMOQ Balanced	12.7
Cassels Blaikie Canadian	12.2
Sceptre Balanced Growth	12.2
Montrusco Select Balanced	12.0
Cormel Balanced	11.9
Capstone Investment Trust	11.8

Source: *BellCharts*, May 1998

Balanced Funds

Balanced funds diversify their investments between stocks and bonds. Typically, 50 to 60 percent of the fund is in usually blue-chip stocks. The rest is invested in government and possibly corporate bonds. These funds provide both growth and income.

Asset allocation funds are balanced funds that invest in a greater variety of stocks and bonds than the typical balanced fund. An asset allocation fund may split its stock investments among Canadian and foreign, large, and small company stocks. On the bond side, it might own Canadian government, corporate, and foreign government bonds. Unlike a typical balanced fund, which generally splits investments relatively equally between stocks and bonds, asset allocation fund managers act according to their own analyses of the markets and potentially overweight a specific area of the market.

Technobabble

When the stock market loses more than ten percent, it's sometimes referred to as a bear market. When the stock market moves higher for a couple of years straight, it's often called a bull market.

Boosting Your Returns Overseas

The Canadian stock market isn't the only game in town. There are stock markets throughout the world. Many foreign corporations are as profitable as their Canadian counterparts. Just look to our friends across the border for some of the most profitable mega-corporations in the world. In addition, some economies in Europe are growing faster than ours.

Over the past ten years, international funds grew at a 11 percent annual average total return. By contrast, the average Canadian stock fund gained 10.9 percent. There are a lot of investment opportunities abroad. That's why it's a good idea to consider investing in a well-managed mutual fund that invests overseas.

As with international bond funds, international stock funds come in all shapes and sizes. Some funds invest in blue-chip stocks around the world. Nestlé, Canon, Hitachi, and Heineken are common holdings in such funds. Others invest in small company stocks worldwide. Funds that invest worldwide, overseas as well as in Canada, are often called global funds. There are funds that invest only in countries outside North America. Some funds invest only in European, Latin American, or Asian companies. Others invest in single countries such as Japan.

A Yen for Investing

You learned about some of the foreign currency risk involved in investing internationally in Chapter 13. Fund managers have to change all their Canadian

Table 14.5 Top-Performing International–Foreign Stock Funds, Average Annual Total Return, 10 Years Ending May 1998

Fund	Average Annual Total Return %
Canada Life US & Int'l Equity	16.7
Trimark Fund	16.7
Templeton Growth Fund	14.9
Sceptre International	14.8
Fidelity Int'l Portfolio	14.4
Saxon World Growth	14.2
MD Growth	13.9
Cornerstone Global	13.1
Desjardins International	12.8
C.I. Global	12.5

Source: *BellCharts*, May 1998

dollars into foreign money, such as the Japanese yen or German mark, before they can buy overseas stocks. Sometimes, Canadian money is exchanged at a rate worse than it was when you put up your dollars to buy it. Even *after* the fund buys overseas stocks, the exchange rate between Canadian dollars and foreign dollars can fluctuate, affecting the value of your fund.

Look Out!

Unless you are a sophisticated investor, avoid funds that invest in a single country. They are not diversified and you are investing in only one country's financial market, so you can lose big-time. A political crisis, government coup, or change in the value of the country's currency can hurt your fund's performance. To avoid these headaches, stick with well-diversified funds that invest worldwide.

Fortunately, fund managers take steps to protect themselves from foreign currency risk. The prospectus will indicate whether the fund manager will hedge against currency fluctuations. Nevertheless, here's a taste of how this foreign currency risk can affect an international fund:

➤ The value of your fund may drop if the foreign currency declines in value against the Canadian dollar.

➤ The value of your fund can rise if the foreign currency increases in value against the Canadian dollar.

Figure 14.1   *Value of $1 invested in the Toronto Stock Exchange 300 Index in 1988.*

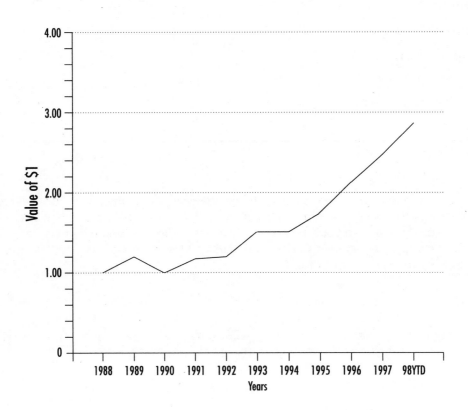

The Least You Need to Know

➤ You invest in stock mutual funds for long-term growth.

➤ Small company stock funds invest in companies that the portfolio manager expects will grow into profitable larger corporations.

➤ Dividend funds invest in blue-chip stocks.

➤ Balanced funds own both stocks and bonds.

Chapter 15

Mutual Funds for Special Situations

> **In This Chapter**
>
> ➤ Risks and rewards of funds that sell at bargain prices
>
> ➤ The funds that invest in specific businesses
>
> ➤ Hedging your investments against inflation

Investing With a Conscience

Got a hankering for something a bit different from the run-of-the-mill stock or bond fund? This chapter delves into even more mutual funds options that are available to those looking for even greater challenges.

For example, there are funds that you can buy for 80 or 90 cents on the dollar. There also are high-risk funds that promise unbelievable profits because they invest in one type of industry. Do you have strong moral and ethical feelings about how companies do business? You have still other funds to choose from! This chapter examines some specialized kinds of mutual funds.

A Different Breed of Mutual Fund Lookalike

Up to this point, you've learned about open-end funds, generally classified as mutual funds. They have no limit as to the number of shares that investors can buy and sell.

There are some other funds known as closed-end funds, which, although frequently grouped with them, are not technically mutual funds. These are also called closed-end investment companies and publicly traded funds. So that you don't get them mixed up with open-end mutual funds, I will refer to closed-end funds as closed-end investment companies. Sometimes you can buy some well-managed, closed-end investment companies for 80 to 90 cents on the dollar.

Open-ended mutual funds continually offer new shares for sale to the investment public. By contrast, closed-end investment companies issue a limited number of shares and do not redeem them. Instead, closed-end shares are traded in the securities markets, with supply and demand determining the price. The closed-end investment company's shares of stock are traded on the securities exchange just like the stock of a corporation. The closed-end investment company's business is managing a portfolio of securities. Some may invest in stocks, bonds, overseas securities, or a combination of securities. There are broadly diversified closed-end investment companies, as well as those that concentrate on a specific industry or group of industries. Some invest in single countries of the world such as Japan, and others invest in regions of the world such as Europe.

There also are dual-purpose, closed-end investment companies that issue two classes of shares. The first class of shares is for investors who want income, and the second class of shares is for those who want growth. You can't buy and sell shares of the closed-end investment company's portfolio. You can only buy or sell the closed-end investment company's stock, which is traded on a stock exchange. The shares of stock easily can be bought or sold through a stockbroker just like any other stock.

Closed-end funds work this way:

➤ You own stock in the closed-end investment company, which manages a portfolio of securities. You buy or sell shares of a closed-end investment company from a brokerage firm.

Technobabble

Closed–end funds are investment companies that sell a fixed number of shares that are traded on the stock exchange. Mutual funds are open–end funds, which means that there is no limit to the number of shares that investors can buy and sell.

➤ Depending on investment objective, a closed-end investment company pays its shareholders distributions in the form of interest, dividends, and capital gains based on the earnings of its portfolio of securities.

➤ The investment company charges a management fee that ranges from about one-half of one percent to 1.5 percent based on the amount of assets in the portfolio. Shareholders can take the distributions in cash or reinvest them and buy more shares of the closed-end investment company.

➤ Do you want to buy a closed-end fund? There are two prices to examine: the investment company's stock price and the net asset value or share price of the closed-end investment company's portfolio of securities. Both are discussed below.

Buy at 80 to 85 Cents on the Dollar

You can find some real bargains when you invest in closed-end investment companies. For example, suppose you talk to a stockbroker (you also can get the information from the stock tables in the newspaper) and find that the stock of the XYZ closed-end investment company sells for $8 per share. Then you check the net asset value of the portfolio of securities managed by the closed-end investment company. It's $10 per share. That means it costs you $8 per share of stock to become a shareholder of an investment company with a portfolio of securities that are priced at $10.

That's a real bargain! Be careful, though. There may be a reason for the discount, including specific economic and/or political conditions. It is always a good idea to consult your investment advisor.

The idea is to buy shares of stock in the closed-end investment company at a discount to the net asset value of the portfolio of securities it manages. You've invested for less than the assets of the investment company are worth. You can buy and hold a well-managed, closed-end investment company for the long haul. Or, you might sell your stock at a profit when it rises in price, and the discount between the share price of the closed-end investment company and net asset value of the portfolio narrows.

Funds for Pure Hearts

Do you have strong feelings about gun control and the arms industry, the environment, pollution, or how workers are treated?

Socially responsible funds do not invest in any old company. These funds have super-strict investment rules. Social funds specifically scout for companies in the alternative energy business or those committed to staying out of the arms or nuclear energy business. They want to invest in companies with great employee benefits. They like firms that don't discriminate against women, minorities, or other groups. They do not invest in tobacco companies, gambling businesses, or alcohol manufacturers.

In Canada, there are 14 mutual funds that select companies to invest in based on social or environmental criteria. They cover Canadian, international, North American and Pacific Rim equities, along with balanced, bond, and small company funds.

Technobabble

Socially responsible funds invest in companies that don't pollute the environment or sell arms. They will not own tobacco or alcohol stocks, nor will they invest in companies with poor employee relations.

115

Great Funds for Ethical Investors

There are four mutual fund companies in Canada that operate as ethical mutual funds:

➤ **Clean Environment Funds**. This is a Toronto-based company that focuses on environmental and waste cleanup firms.

➤ **Desjardins Environment Fund.** This group is sponsored by Desjardins Trust, a subsidiary of the Quebec-based Desjardins system of caisses populaires, and invests in "environmentally conscious Canadian corporations."

➤ **Ethical Funds**. Owned and controlled by the Canadian credit union system, Ethical Funds runs eight different funds. Ethical Funds screens companies for industrial relations, racial equality, tobacco, military production, nuclear energy, and environmental practices.

➤ **Investors Summa Fund**. Investors Group, the largest mutual fund company in Canada, runs this fund. The Summa Fund screens for alcohol, tobacco, gambling, military weapons, pornography, environmental policies, and repressive regimes.

The Least You Need to Know

➤ A closed-end fund can trade at a discount to the NAV (net asset value).

➤ Socially responsible funds are a great alternative for ethically minded investors.

Part 4
The One-Hour-a-Year Investment Plans

Picking a mutual fund to buy, unfortunately, is not the end of the line when it comes to investing. You need to keep on top of your fund's performance. Is it up or down as much as similar funds? Is it a dud?

Yet, if you're like most of us, you don't have time to manage your investments. It's no wonder! How can you possibly stay on top of all the wheeling and dealing on the markets when you have to work full time and raise a family?

Mutual funds help make it easy to invest. This part of The Complete Idiot's Guide to Making Money with Mutual Funds makes it even easier. You'll learn easy ways to evaluate your mutual fund's performance, and you'll find out tried-and-true strategies you can use to get the best mileage out of your investments with the least amount of time and worry.

Chapter 16

How 'Ya Doing?

> **In This Chapter**
>
> ➤ Evaluating a fund's performance
>
> ➤ Is your mix of funds up to snuff?
>
> ➤ When should you bail out?

Even though you've probably selected the right mutual funds for you by now, you're not quite finished with the exercise of setting up your investment portfolio. It's always a good idea to stay on top of your financial situation—you want to be sure your mutual funds are doing what they say they're supposed to do: make money.

This chapter reviews ways to monitor your mutual fund performance. You'll learn how to evaluate how your fund is doing and whether you should sell your fund and buy a new one.

Your Mutual Fund Checkup

You've got a couple of funds. Now what?

With a car, you get an oil change about every four months. Once a year, you take it in for a tune-up. Mutual funds are no different. You should give your funds a financial checkup on a regular basis.

Hot Tip

Have a computer? You can buy software that keeps track of your investments. Quicken and Microsoft Money can help you get your finances in order.

Check on them daily and you'll drive yourself bonkers. On the other hand, you don't want to be an ostrich. If you bury your head in the sand and forget about your fund, much can change. A portfolio manager's hot hands can turn into ice cubes. If you are using a discount broker you definitely should be monitoring your funds more closely than if you are employing a full-service investment advisor.

If you've done your homework and invested in funds with good long-term track records, you probably can rest assured that your funds will grow in value over the years.

You might not own the number-one fund for the year but, based on your investment comfort level, you want your funds to lose less in down markets and do well compared with similar funds over three-year, five-year, and ten-year periods.

There are more than 1800 mutual funds. The odds of investing in next year's top-performing fund are equivalent to your chances of winning the Kentucky Derby.

Remember, though, with mutual funds, just because you didn't cash in a winning ticket doesn't mean you forfeit bragging rights.

When you do your checkup, it's best to compare your fund's returns with similar funds. Look at the average annual total return of the entire group of funds over the last three months, one year, three years, and five years.

Some of the resources available to track your mutual funds include: the financial section of the newspaper, the library, and the Internet. A great Web site that connects you to all the major fund companies is The Fund Library at www.fundlibrary.com

Here's what to do once you've looked up the information:

1. Ask yourself, "What was my fund's total return this year to date compared with the total returns on similar funds and the fund group average?" Compare the average annual total returns on your fund to similar funds and the peer group average over the past one-year, three-year, or five-year periods.

2. You also can compare your fund's total returns to the market averages this year to date and over one-, three-, or five-year periods. The TSE 300 is an index that shows the performance of a large group of stocks in Canada. If you have an international stock fund, you can compare it to the Europe, Australia, and Far East Index (EAFE), which tracks stocks listed on major world stock exchanges. The Standard and Poor 500 is the typical U.S. stock fund benchmark.

   Use the Scotia McLeod Bond Index to compare your fund's performance based on total return. This index tells you how the bond market is performing so that you can see how your funds stack up against the performance of the bond market.

3. Subtract the total return on your fund from the average peer groups' return. You also can subtract the return from the market averages. If the difference is positive, your fund is doing better than other funds. If it's negative, you're doing worse. You can use the Fund Performance Worksheet to get started comparing funds.

Table 16.1 Fund Performance Worksheet

Your Fund	Your Fund's Total Return %	Peer Group or Other Funds' Return % (Subtract from Your Fund's Return %)	Difference

Create a worksheet like this one to compare your fund's performance with similar funds.

Let's take the fictitious ABC Growth Fund, a no-load growth fund. Assume you owned the fund for five years. Over the past five years ending in June 1998, the ABC Growth Fund had an annual average total return of 11.25 percent. The TSE 300 had a 11 percent annual average total return, and the average growth fund a 10.46 percent annual average total return over the same period. So, over the past five years, the ABC Growth Fund earned .25 percentage points annually more than the stock market average and .79 percent points annually more than the average growth stock fund.

Not too shabby. But what's ABC done more recently? Year to date, for the first six months of 1998, the fund's total return was 6.9 percent. By contrast, over this period, the average growth fund's total return was 7.4 percent, and the TSE 300's total return was 10.8 percent.

Does this mean you should sell the ABC Growth Fund because it lagged behind these indices over the first six months of the year? Nope. You know it's been a

121

winner over the past five years, even though it's lagged behind over the past six months. In a half-year or year's time, even a good fund can trail others.

You know your stock or bond funds are doing particularly well when they beat their market averages. Don't forget—with your fund, you're paying management fees, and some of your fund's holdings are kept in cash. Indexes, such as the TSE 300, don't reflect these factors.

How Does the Fund Rank Against Others?

You also can check newspapers, magazines, or even the fund's financial reports for information on how your fund compares to funds with the same investment objectives over several time periods. Chapter 9 discusses the annual, semi-annual, or quarterly financial reports unitholders receive from their fund. Look for how your fund stacks up against funds with the same investment objective—and market averages, such as the TSE 300.

Depending upon which publication you pick up, the fund's *ranking* may be expressed either as a number or coded percentile. A numerical ranking provides a number show-

Sidelines

There are a couple of other items to check besides performance. Look at your fund's latest financial report or call your advisor and get information about the following:

Are there major changes in the fund's holdings? Has the fund manager put more of the fund in small company stocks? Has he or she loaded up in one industry or diversified among many industries? Has the fund manager changed? (If the fund manager is new, you may want to investigate his history and/or experience.) This information, along with current performance, gives you a feel for how the fund is being managed.

If you own a bond fund, check to see whether there has been a major change, such as a change in the average bond ratings of the fund's holdings or a change in the average maturity of the fund. If a bond fund's average credit rating has dropped—for example, from AA to A— and the average maturity has lengthened, it means the fund manager is taking on more risk to earn higher returns. By contrast, if the average credit rating has increased and the average maturity has shortened, the bond fund manager may be playing it safe.

ing how the fund did relative to other funds or funds with the same investment objective. The percentile ranking explains in which percentile of funds your fund ranks. Listings may compare your fund with all mutual funds. They also can compare your fund to funds with the same investment objective. A fund in, for instance, the top quartile ranks in the top 25 percent of its class.

Why Do Funds Lose Steam?

Why would a fund with a good long-term track record suddenly fall behind? Its stock-picking style may be out of favour. Growth fund managers may lag behind because bargain-priced, undervalued stocks are in favour. By contrast, a couple of years down the road, growth stocks, which tend to show 25 percent to 30 percent annual earnings growth, may be in and undervalued stocks out.

Funds that have too much money in cash instead of stocks may trail the overall stock market and stock funds that are fully invested in a bull market. The fund's manager may have misjudged the direction of the stock market and kept money in cash as a safe haven. As a result, the manager may have just 70 percent to 80 percent of the fund's holdings invested in stocks when the market moves higher.

Plain old lousy stock picks are another reason a fund may do poorly. The fund manager's evaluation of a company, an industry, or the economy could be off the mark.

Bad timing can also be a factor. The companies a fund owns could look good on paper, but the darned stock price doesn't move. For some unexplained reason, there could be more sellers than buyers of the stocks the fund happens to own.

Does this mean you should dump your fund? No. You must look at several factors before you decide when to sell.

When to Sell Your Funds

When should you sell your fund? If your fund has been underperforming for one or two years—don't sell it in haste. Instead, start asking some questions, along the lines of the points covered in this chapter. Consult your investment advisor and ask his or her opinion. Stock returns tend to move in cycles. It definitely could be time to make a change if your fund underperforms similar funds over at least a five-year period.

You should also consider changing funds under the following conditions:

➤ Your fund manager has a good track record and then leaves.

➤ The fund changes its investment objective.

➤ The fund merges with another fund that has a mediocre track record.

➤ Your own financial condition or tolerance for risk has changed.

123

Evaluating Your Fund Picks

What if you own several different types of funds?

You have to look at the total return on your investment and compare it to a similar type of benchmark. Suppose that you have 50 percent of your investment in a growth stock fund that registers a total return of ten percent for the year and 50 percent in a bond fund that has a total return of six percent for the year. Figure your investment's total return for the year by following these steps:

1. Multiply .50 by 10 percent, the total return on your growth stock fund for the year. That equals 5 percent.

2. Multiply .50 by 6 percent, the total return of your bond fund for the year. That equals 3 percent.

3. Add the total returns that represent the growth fund and bond fund's share of your portfolio: 5 percent plus 3 percent equals 8 percent. This represents a weighted average total return on your entire portfolio.

Now you have to compare that to a couple of benchmarks, such as having 50 percent invested in the TSE 300 and 50 percent invested in the Scotia McLeod Bond Index, to see how well you did versus the market averages. Suppose the TSE 300 total return for the year was 9.5 percent and the Scotia McLeod Bond Index total return was 5.8 percent. Fifty percent of 9.5 percent equals 4.75 percent. Fifty percent of 5.8 percent equals 2.9 percent for a combined total return of 7.65 percent.

To see how your investment mix did against the market averages, subtract 7.65 percent, the combined total return of the market averages, from 8 percent, the combined total return of your funds. The result is 0.35 percent.

Your mix of mutual funds gave you some extra return over the appropriate benchmarks, which reflect the market averages. If your mix of funds underperformed the benchmarks by a wide margin, it may be an indication that you might want to consider selling those funds and find funds that perform better. You also can use this method to compare the combined total return of your investment mix with similar funds or the fund's investment objective averages.

The Least You Need to Know

➤ Compare your fund's performance with similar funds, the average of funds with the same investment objective, and indexes, such as the TSE 300 index.

➤ If your fund is underperforming by a small margin, give it a chance—start asking the tough questions.

➤ Use the mutual fund tables available in the newspaper or through several reporting services to monitor your fund's performance annually.

➤ Consider selling your fund if it underperforms similar funds over three to five years.

Chapter 17

Getting Rich a Little Bit at a Time: Dollar Cost Averaging

In This Chapter

➤ Investing regularly

➤ Starting a savings program

➤ The best kinds of funds for dollar cost averaging

Well, people, you have a choice. You can read the paper daily, sweat out all the market's hiccups, and try to sell when you think your mutual fund's share price has peaked. Unfortunately, most of us don't know when that's actually going to happen, so there's a good chance you also can miss out on some big profits this way.

Your other option is to just sit tight and play it cool. This chapter focuses on one investment strategy that enables you to do the latter. You merely invest a certain amount of money regularly. This way, some of your cash is invested at high share prices, and some at lower share prices. Even though many of us have been doing this same type of thing for years with our plain old bank savings account, the gurus have a fancy name for this style of investing—*dollar cost averaging*.

With dollar cost averaging, you can build your wealth in a systematic level-headed manner. You don't have to watch every single move the market makes. You don't need an MBA or PhD either. This chapter goes into the pluses and minuses of dollar cost averaging, which is one of the simplest ways to invest.

A Piggy Bank for Grown-Ups

With dollar cost averaging, you invest $50 or $100, for example, every month into the mutual fund of your choice. Whether you're saving for your child's future education, a vacation home, or your retirement, this is a low-risk way to invest.

Usually, any interest and dividends paid by your mutual funds will be reinvested automatically. When you do that, your earnings also buy more shares of your fund each month. Or, you can request that you receive these earnings in cash.

With dollar cost averaging, there's no need to worry if the fund's share price drops. When this happens, your regular monthly investment, plus any earnings, is purchasing new shares of the mutual fund at the lower prices. Look at the value of your fund a few years after doing this, once the price rises again, and you'll be in for a shock—a pleasant one!

Most firms that sell mutual funds can help you dollar cost average through some of the services they provide. Most have automatic investment savings plans. You can have the money automatically taken out of your chequing account and invested in the fund of your choice before you have a chance to miss it. Ask your investment advisor or financial planner for details.

Taking the Guesswork out of It

Dollar cost averaging takes the guesswork out of investing. When you dollar cost average, you don't have to worry about timing the markets. You are always buying shares. Because you always have money invested, you profit during periods in which a fund's price rises. Other times, the share price may decline. But like a squirrel accumulating nuts for the winter, you are accumulating units. Then when the fund's unit price rises, your investment is worth more.

How Dollar Cost Averaging Works

Suppose you invest $100 each month in a stock fund that sells at $20 per share. You invest $100 and receive five units. The market drops and the fund's unit price drops to

$10 per unit. You again invest your $100. At $10 per unit you receive 10 units for your $100. Let's assume by the next month, the market has returned to where it was when you started and your fund is now selling at $20 per unit. You now receive five units for your $100 investment. Table 18.1 shows what your investment looks like.

You own 20 units of the fund in which you invested $300. Your units are worth more than what you paid. The *average price per unit* was $16.67. The average cost was $15.00 because you invested $300 and bought a total of 20 units.

Hot Tip

Automatic investment plans are great for investors who don't have a lot of disposable income. With most mutual funds, all you need is a minimum of $25 a month!

Table 17.1 How Dollar Cost Averaging Works

Month	Regular Investment	Unit Price	Units Acquired
Month 1	$100	$20	5
Month 2	$100	$10	10
Month 3	$100	$20	5
Total	$300	—	20

Average Unit Cost: $15.00 ($300 divided by 20 units)

Average Unit Price: $16.67

The idea behind dollar cost averaging is to invest for the longer term. You have to invest through thick and thin, sticking with a fund in down markets. If you bail out early, you can be forced to sell units at a loss.

The Downside

There are some things that you should be aware of with a dollar cost averaging strategy. This type of investment strategy may not be for everyone. If you are an aggressive investor who can tolerate a big drop in total return in return for long-term growth, you may want to invest a lump sum.

Dollar cost averaging can lose its effectiveness over time. If the same amount is invested each month, the money you've accumulated may not go as far as you thought when you consider inflation or the increasing costs of necessities. As a result, you

127

Look Out!

Don't dollar cost average all your spare cash. Even with dollar cost averaging, there's never a guarantee that your fund will rebound from a few bad years. If you pick the wrong fund, the money you invest over the years may not grow to what you expected.

should consider increasing your monthly investment each year by $25 or $50, for example, to keep up with rising inflation.

Second, there are no rules to tell you when to sell after you've used dollar cost averaging for a number of years. There are no guarantees that the average cost of the fund units you bought over the years will be less than the market price of the fund when you sell. To make dollar cost averaging work, you have to pick the right time to sell the fund.

Third, if you're just starting out with dollar cost averaging, you might find it hard to invest in a fund at bargain prices. Bull markets can last twice as long as bear markets. Most of the time, you'll buy fund units at higher prices. One solution is to invest twice as much in your fund during bear markets.

Fourth, if you invest a lump sum in a fund, you have more money working for you at the beginning, compared with stashing away a little bit every month. Over the long haul, the lump sum investment grows much more. Of course, if you don't have much money in the first place, dollar cost averaging is better than nothing at all.

Finding the Best Funds

Dollar cost averaging works well with all types of stock funds, ranging from aggressive growth and small company stocks to tried-and-true balanced funds. It works best with more volatile funds—the ones that drop and then soar in value. If you invest in a fund with a good long-term track record that also sports some volatility in unit values, you've found a great fund for dollar cost averaging. Even Nervous Nellies can cheer when the fund loses money. Why? You're buying more units of the fund at a lower price. When it rebounds, you build up a tidy sum. Use this tactic over the years, and dollar cost averaging will serve you well.

When shopping for a mutual fund to use in a dollar cost averaging investment plan, consider the following:

➤ The ideal dollar cost averaging candidate should have outperformed its peers over the longer term. You want a fund with a good long-term track record. Look at the fund's annual rate of return over at least a five-year period. Then look at the fund's return from year to year. You want to invest in funds that have performed as well as or better than similar funds over the long term.

➤ The fund should have shown a proven ability to bounce back from bad years such as 1973, 1979, 1981, 1987, 1990, and 1994.

➤ Most minimum investment dollar amounts are waived if you set up an automatic purchase plan.

The Worst Funds

Some funds are better dollar cost averaging candidates than others. If you dollar cost average into money market funds or shorter-term bond funds, you accumulate money that earns a lower rate of interest. With these kinds of funds you're saving, not investing. Dollar cost averaging also won't build your wealth as much in a balanced fund or income fund as it will in a growth fund. To make dollar cost averaging work best, you need to invest in more aggressive funds that have the ability to grow.

For those who are nervous about socking away money in an aggressive growth or growth fund, consult Chapter 19. You'll learn about some low-risk ways to dollar cost average into stock funds to build your retirement nest egg.

What about bond funds?

Dollar cost averaging can work with long-term bond funds. When interest rates rise or fall one percent, most long-term bond funds can move down or up in value about ten to 12 percent. Over the past ten years, long-term bond funds have grown at an annual rate of close to ten percent. If you invested $1200 through thick and thin in your bond fund for each of the past ten years, your money grew to almost $20,000. Not bad!

Getting Started with Dollar Cost Averaging

Even before you start dollar cost averaging, as you learned in Chapter 2, you need to make sure that you have money socked away to meet financial emergencies. That money should be put in a low-risk investment such as a savings account or money market fund. You need to establish your goals and determine your investment mix based on your tolerance for risk as shown in your answers to the quiz in Chapter 6.

Dollar cost averaging should begin only after you develop a financial cushion for emergencies and determine that you're willing to take on a little more risk in exchange for building your long-term wealth. Then you can pick a fund for dollar cost averaging.

First start saving regularly in a bank account until you have a regular stream of income going into that account. Then you can start by investing as little as $25 a month. But

129

there is no upper limit on what you can sock away regularly. Once you decide how much you want to invest, there are several ways to go about it.

1. You can write a cheque and send it to your fund company or investment advisor each month. That way you can increase or decrease your investments as time goes by. You also can skip a payment if you have a financial emergency. What's the drawback to this method? You need to make sure you have the discipline to invest every month.

2. You can sign up for the fund's automatic investment plan, as discussed in Chapter 11. That way you don't have to do anything. It's taken care of for you. If you need to make changes in the amount you want to invest, you can always call your investment advisor or fund company. The drawback? You've got to be sure you keep a balance in your chequing account large enough to cover your monthly investment. Otherwise, you might find yourself overdrawn and face extra charges for bounced cheques. That's a no-no.

The Least You Need to Know

➤ With dollar cost averaging, you invest every month for the long term.

➤ You can invest as little as $25 a month though a mutual fund's automatic investment program. Ask your investment advisor for details.

➤ Dollar cost averaging takes the guesswork out of investing.

➤ It takes a few years for dollar cost averaging to work. You have to accumulate enough units to benefit from the growth of the fund.

Chapter 18

Keeping an Even Keel: Diversification and Portfolio Rebalancing

---

In This Chapter

➤ Getting better returns with less risk

➤ An investment program that takes just an hour a year

➤ When to adjust your investment mix

We live in a paranoid society when it comes to money. The result is that most people oversave and underinvest. They sock too much away in the bank and not enough in stocks or bonds.

The reason for this paranoia is that nobody, quite understandably, wants to lose their hard-earned cash. Ironically, years later when that money is really needed to live on, it's the paranoid crew that finds they don't have as much as they'd like. True, they might have succeeded in preserving their principal; but, meanwhile, everything they buy costs more. Their low-risk invested money doesn't go quite far enough.

This chapter looks at a low-risk way to invest in mutual funds so that you might avoid this shock later on in life. You'll learn how to manage an investment mix that always matches your tolerance for risk. You'll also learn how to combine dollar cost averaging with the taking of profits to boost the return on your mutual fund investments.

Balancing Your Act

Keeping your investment balanced means diversifying your mutual fund investments by owning different types of mutual funds that invest in different types of assets, such as stocks, bonds, and cash. Stock funds, bond funds, and money market funds don't always perform in tandem with each other. So, if a stock fund's total return has declined, the losses may be offset by the total return on the bond fund and money market fund. As mentioned earlier in the book, spreading your assets over a variety of different investments is important. If you diversify your mutual fund portfolio, your investment performance should fluctuate less because losses from some investments are offset by gains in others. As a result, you have less risk than if you were to put all the money into one type of investment, such as a stock fund or bond fund.

In addition to lowering the risks, diversification can offer higher total returns than you would expect from investments in only the most conservative types of mutual funds, such as money market funds.

I think diversification makes a lot of sense because no one type of mutual fund performs best in all types of economic conditions. No one can predict which fund will register high total returns in the future. That's why it's important to diversify. For example, if you have a diversified portfolio of mutual funds, a decline in the value of your bond fund could be offset by an increase in the total return of an international stock fund that invests overseas.

Diversification alone, however, may not be enough to keep you on a steady course. What happens if your stock fund registers high total returns for a couple of years running? You may find you have too much money in stocks based on your tolerance for risk. That's where portfolio rebalancing comes into play.

Technobabble

When you *rebalance* your funds, you periodically adjust the mix of your portfolio to keep targeted percentages of your overall investment dollars in each of your funds, based on your risk tolerance.

Rebalancing Your Act

What is rebalancing? Remember those seesaws at the school playground? The idea was to keep it level. If one kid was too high, the other was too low. The kid on the side closest to the ground had to push up to bring a buddy on the other side down from his or her lofty perch.

Rebalancing your investments works the same way. Sometimes your stock funds shoot up in value and your bond fund or other funds decline in value, so you have to balance things.

In a bull market, such as 1996–97, when the average Canadian large-cap stock fund shot up more than 40 percent (one-year return ending July 1997), you might have found yourself with too much invested in stock funds at the end of the year.

If you get into a bear market, you want to keep your losses to a minimum. It's important to take some of your profits and make some readjustments to your mix of mutual funds at least once a year.

Look Out!

Avoid rebalancing with funds that charge front-end or back-end loads. Every time you exit the fund, you're stuck paying a fee. You wind up just paying your stockbroker or investment company commissions.

In Chapter 6 you learned your risk tolerance, the types of funds you should invest in, and how to slice your investment pie to get the best returns with the least amount of risk.

When you rebalance your funds, you go one step further. You examine your portfolio and make adjustments to ensure your investment mix has remained proportionally the same as when you originally diversified.

For example, suppose you set up your portfolio with 60 percent invested in stock funds and 40 percent in bond funds and/or money market funds. You're earning a decent return and are sleeping well at night. Now what happens if stock prices surge into a bull market? At the end of the year, you look at what your investments are worth, and discover that you now have 75 percent of your money in stock funds and only 25 percent in bond funds and/or money market funds.

Whoa! That's too risky.

What do you do? You simply adjust your mix so that you have 60 percent stock funds and 40 percent bond funds again. Now you can resume your eight hours of shut-eye every night. When you readjust your mix of funds, you sell some units of your stock fund and invest the profits in the bond funds. That way you maintain the same percentage of money invested in each stock fund to match your tolerance for risk.

The Advantages

There are several benefits to rebalancing your mutual fund portfolio:

➤ You're keeping track of your investments. Rebalancing your portfolio forces you to check the performance of your funds periodically.

➤ You're maintaining a risk level that's comfortable for you. You have evaluated your tolerance for risk and determined that you are an aggressive, moderate, or conservative investor. As a result, you don't want your mutual fund portfolio to get too far out of line. For example, if you are a conservative investor who is comfortable with a 50 percent investment in a stock fund, you don't want to see the value of the stock fund investment become a major proportion of your portfolio. Then you'll have too much money at risk.

➤ You're buying low and selling high. Similarly, you are taking profits from funds that have increased in unit value.

The Disadvantages

Yes, there really are disadvantages to rebalancing your mutual fund portfolio.

➤ If you rebalance funds outside your retirement plan, you'll pay taxes on your profits. After paying Revenue Canada, your returns may not be that spectacular. Of course, there are ways to minimize your taxes when you invest outside of a tax-deferred retirement savings account. You can invest in stock funds with low portfolio turnover. These funds do not distribute a lot of capital gains to share-holders because they buy and hold the securities in the portfolio. As a result, shareholders may pay less taxes on fund distributions. You also can invest in low-dividend-yielding stock funds. These are funds that invest primarily in small company stocks. Smaller companies plow their profits back into the company and don't pay shareowners dividends. You won't pay much in taxes if the fund does not earn a lot of dividends.

➤ If, however, you are investing new money each year, you can use these funds (for example, growth and dividend funds) to rebalance your portfolio, thereby eliminating the need to sell units (and bypassing Revenue Canada in the process).

➤ You could get out of your stock fund too early and miss out on higher returns over the years.

Best Types of Funds to Rebalance

Before you start rebalancing, you first need to make sure you select funds that make different types of investments. That way when one is down, the other may be up a bit. It all helps.

Refer back to Chapter 7 for guidelines on the percentages to invest in stock, bond, and money funds. Keep the number of funds between two and ten so that it's easier to rebalance your portfolio.

To refresh your memory, younger folks who haven't retired yet probably should pick funds among these categories: aggressive growth funds, balanced funds, international stock funds, and bond or money market funds.

Retired folks should limit their fund categories largely to balanced funds, bond funds or a dividend stock fund, and money market funds.

No matter what age you are, it's important to diversify. By rebalancing, you have an easy-to-use formula of when to buy and sell. It's always best to rebalance your portfolio in a tax-deferred investment such as an RRSP, company pension, or life insurance policy that lets you invest in mutual funds.

How Frequently Do You Do It?

Nervous Nellies can rebalance their investment mixes every six months. Generally, though, it's best to give it at least 12 months for a couple of reasons:

➤ If you make frequent changes, you have to pay taxes on your profitable trades— unless the funds are in an RRSP or other kind of tax-deferred investment.

➤ Make frequent changes, and you could get whipsawed. In other words, the funds you're reinvesting in might change direction quickly. Unfortunately, it's possible to rebalance, take your profits, and reinvest in poorer-performing funds. You could be reinvesting at higher prices than you should.

➤ The longer you wait, the less frequently you have to figure out how much to invest in each fund. You want to limit your time as money manager to one hour a year, if possible.

➤ The longer you wait, the more time your money has to grow. You want to reap the benefits of rising stock prices without feeling as if you're taking on too much risk. One year, history tells us, seems like a nice compromise.

Getting It to Work

Let's look at how rebalancing worked from 1986 through 1994 based on the performance of a growth fund and a government bond fund. Our hypothetical example assumes that distributions are reinvested. Taxes were not taken into account.

Suppose you invested $1500 in a growth fund and $1000 in a government bond fund at the beginning of 1986. Your mix was 60 percent stocks and 40 percent bonds. You readjusted once a year.

You can use more funds if you want an extra layer of diversification, but let's keep it simple. See Table 18.1 for an example of rebalancing your funds, keeping 60 percent of the dollars in growth funds and 40 percent in government bond funds.

The table shows how your money will grow if you rebalance at the end of each year, assuming that 60 percent is invested in a growth fund and 40 percent is invested in a bond fund at the beginning of the following year. Fund distributions are reinvested, but taxes are not taken into consideration. Remember, past performance is no indication of future results. This is a hypothetical example to show you how it works. Your total returns may be different in the future.

Column 1 of the table lists the year-end period of the hypothetical study. Column 2 shows the total value at year-end of the growth fund investment, and Column 3 shows the bond fund's total value at year-end. The last column shows the combined total value of both funds.

At the end of each year, you multiply the combined total value of the portfolio by 60 percent to get the amount you should invest at the beginning of the next year in the growth fund.

Table 18.1 Rebalancing Your Funds

Year Ending	Total Growth Fund $	Total Bond Fund $	Portfolio Total $
1986	$1,725	$1,120	$2,845
1987	1,758	1,149	2,908
1988	2,005	1,244	3,250
1989	2,476	1,456	3,932
1990	2,241	1,698	3,939
1991	3,237	1,795	5,032
1992	3,260	2,133	5,993
1993	3,744	2,407	6,151
1994	3,616	2,361	5,997
Mid-year 1995	4,124	2,653	6,339

You did pretty well from 1986 through mid-1995. Your $2500 investment grew to $6339 by keeping a mix of 60 percent in a growth fund and 40 percent in a stock fund every year.

Once every year, you totaled up the value of both investments. Then you put 60 percent of the total into your growth fund and 40 percent in your bond fund.

Stock and bond funds had some pretty good years since 1986. Your stock fund lost five percent in 1990 and two percent in 1994. The bond fund lost just four percent in 1994. In the future, the returns may be different, so don't count on earning the same amount as the example over the next several years.

It's important that when your investments were up, you took profits. When they were down, you bought more shares at lower prices. The end result was positive. In 1990, for example, your growth stock fund lost five percent, and the bond fund gained eight percent. At the end of the year you remixed. As a result, you invested a few bucks more in your growth stock fund at the start of 1991.

Voila! In 1991, your stock fund gained a whopping 37 percent.

Look what happened by mid-year 1994 following losses in both stocks and bonds in the previous year. Your stock fund lost two percent in 1994 but, by mid-year 1995, it was up 15 percent.

Your bond fund lost four percent in 1994 but, by mid-year 1995, the fund was up 11 percent.

How do you keep tabs on your funds so you can rebalance? It's easy. At the end of every year, for example, you look at the combined total value of your mutual fund portfolio. Then you slice the pie appropriately. For example, suppose you keep 70 percent in a stock fund, 20 percent in a bond fund, and 10 percent in a money fund. The total value of your portfolio at the end of the year is $10,000. To rebalance, take 70 percent of $10,000 to get $7000, or the amount you should have invested in your stock fund. Twenty percent of $10,000 ($2000) is the amount you should have invested in a bond fund, and 10 percent of $10,000 ($1000) is the amount you should have invested in a money market fund. Once you have the right amounts for each fund, tell your investment advisor or broker how much you want in each fund. The investment advisor will make the exchanges among the funds to bring you into balance. With most mutual funds, as long as you stay within the same fund family, there are no costs to switch.

Hot Tip

Be sure to check the confirmation statements that are sent to you by the fund group after you make your trades. You want to make sure it follows your instructions to a "T."

The Least You Need to Know

➤ Diversify your investment mix to match your risk tolerance.

➤ Rebalancing means always replenishing your funds to retain the same percentage mix at the begining of each year.

➤ Rebalancing is a low-risk way to invest.

➤ Rebalancing lets you take profits in winning investments and dollar cost average into underperforming investments.

➤ Rebalancing works best in retirement savings plans because you don't pay taxes on the trades.

Part 5
Financial Planning

By now, we hope you've grasped some of the basics of mutual fund investing. Despite all we've been through together so far, all this information is only the tip of the iceberg. Once you make all this money, you have to deal with Revenue Canada.

Then there are all those reasons you wanted to invest, remember? You need money for retirement and to finance your child's post-secondary education. You also need to plan for your loved ones' needs when you die.

This part of the book shows you how to deal with all the heavy-duty stuff that comes after you've picked out your mutual funds. You'll learn how to figure out what you owe in taxes, and some good ways to cut your tax bill. You'll also learn how to help get Junior—financially, at least—through university. Then, if there's any money left over, you'll find out how to plan for your own happy and healthy retirement.

Chapter 19

Tax-Sheltered Plans for the Entire Family: RRSPs, RRIFs, and RESPs

In This Chapter

➤ Registered Retirement Savings Plans (RRSPs)

➤ Registered Retirement Income Funds (RRIFs)

➤ Registered Education Savings Plans (RESPs)

Alright folks, now that you are experts on how to buy mutual funds, it's time to look at the benefits of investing in mutual funds inside tax-sheltered plans. Tax-sheltered plans are a must for any investor and are one of the few tax-deferral vehicles left to Canadians.

Start early and invest often. Say this to yourself ten times. The best way to build savings is to put time to work and harness the power of compounding. For instance, if at age twenty, you put $100 a month into a tax-sheltered plan until you reached age sixty-five, assuming a 10 percent annual compound rate of return, you'd be a millionaire by the time you retired!

Taxes, Taxes, Taxes

Canadians are burdened with taxes almost everywhere we turn. There's income tax, property tax, provincial sales tax, goods and services tax, tax on interest income, capital gains tax... the list goes on and on. Unfortunately, there are very few tax breaks available today. So, you should make full use of the tax-sheltered plans that the government offers while you can.

The RRSP: King of Tax-Sheltered Plans

One of the best tax-sheltered plans available to Canadians today is the Registered Retirement Savings Plan, or what's more commonly called the RRSP. An RRSP is not an investment like a mutual fund or stock, but an account that you put your money in. Inside the RRSP account, you can buy and sell different investments tax-free.

The RRSP was designed in 1957 for people who were not covered by a company-sponsored retirement plan to help them save for retirement. The Government of Canada encourages Canadians to save for their retirement and has developed tax incentives for those who do invest an RRSP.

Hot Tip

The RRSP is definitely long term and the crux of all retirement planning. With time on your side, you can see your investment grow substantially. Remember, doing something (something smart, that is) is better than doing nothing!

Technobabble

An RRSP is a Registered Retirement Savings Plan. It's not an investment like a stock or bond but, rather, an account where you can buy and sell different investments tax free.

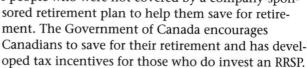

The beauty of an RRSP is that it is a tax-sheltered investment vehicle. The amount you contribute annually to your RRSP, within your maximum allowable contribution limits, is completely tax-deductible. In many cases, you can expect a significant tax reduction. For example, if you are in a 50 percent tax bracket, a $10,000 contribution to your RRSP would mean a $5000 reduction in taxes paid. Even better—the investment income earned inside an RRSP (interest, dividends, capital gains) is sheltered from current taxes. Your money grows more quickly in an RRSP because, unlike a conventional investment account, your money compounds tax free.

Once you have set up your RRSP account at your bank, brokerage firm, or mutual fund company, you are allowed to make an annual contribution of up to $13,500 or 18 percent of your earned income for that year, whichever is less. These contribution limits may change in the future—make sure you know what the limits are. If you are covered by another retirement plan, such as your company pension plan, you can contribute to an RRSP, provided your pension has not exceeded your RRSP contribution limit. Any excess RRSP contribution room may then be used. You may contribute to an RRSP until you reach age sixty-nine. At that point, you can take the cash or you must convert your RRSP either to a RRIF (Registered Retirement Income Fund) or to an

Sidelines

RRSP Contribution Limits (Note: These limits may change in the future.)

The previous year's unused contribution room (to 1991) plus:

- 18 percent of last year's earned income to a maximum of $13,500

OR

- If you hold a pension plan, 18 percent of last year's earned income to a maximum of $13,500 minus last year's pension adjustment.

Keep in mind that your RRSP contributions must come from "earned income," such as from your salary. You should receive a Notice of Assessment from the government stating the maximum amount you are allowed to contribute to your RRSP.

annuity, which requires you to withdraw a minimum amount each year. But more on that later.

To allow for any unintentional overcontributions (i.e., beyond the legislated limit) to your RRSP, each individual can have up to $2000 in overcontributions without paying a penalty tax. Any overcontributions in excess of this $2000 are subject to a 1 percent per month penalty. If you do not make your maximum RRSP contribution in a given year, according to current legislation, you may "carry forward" indefinitely the unused portion accumulated since 1991.

When you do withdraw money from your RRSP, you pay taxes at your current rate. For most people, money will be withdrawn at retirement when income tends to be lower and, therefore, personal tax rates may be lower. If, however, you withdraw money from your RRSP earlier than age sixty-nine, you will be penalized a withholding tax (at 10 percent or more, depending on the amount withdrawn), and you will pay income tax on the withdrawn amount at your current rate.

Let's say your earned income for last year was $30,000 and you are 30 years old. Your maximum RRSP contribution for this year would then be 18 percent x $30,000, which is $5400. You put that $5400 maximum into your RRSP account for this year, and at least this much for the next thirty-five years (provided your earned income is at least $30,000 over this time period and the limits remain the same). Assuming an 8 percent annual compound rate of return, you'd have well over a million dollars at age 65! Remember—invest early, invest often!

Foreign Content in Your RRSP

One more critical thing to note regarding RRSPs. The maximum amount of foreign content you can hold in your RRSP is 20 percent. Foreign content means any investing you do outside Canada—for example, U.S. stocks, European bonds, or an Asian-Pacific mutual fund. It is a good idea to maximize your foreign content because it helps you to diversify your investments outside Canada. Remember—don't put all your eggs in one basket! If you have approximately 80 percent of your portfolio exposed to Canada, you can maximize your foreign content and expose your portfolio to the opportunities that exist in the rest of the world. Be careful not to exceed the 20 percent foreign content as there is a monthly penalty of
1 percent per month on any amount that exceeds the 20 percent limit.

Hot Tip

Your annual RRSP contribution deadline is March 1.

When Are My RRSP Contributions Due?

Each year there is a RRSP contribution deadline, which usually falls on March 1. Any contributions made before that deadline can be used for the previous year's tax return (assuming there is available room to make the contribution). Many people wait until the last minute to make their contribution and many times will not have enough money to maximize their contribution. They end up taking out a loan (you should be able to get an RRSP loan at prime as long as you will pay it back over one year) and paying interest on the loan.

There's a better way. Each month you should be allocating a set portion of your pay-

Hot Tip

Don't wait until the last minute—such as March 1 or your sixty-eighth birthday—to make your RRSP contribution. The earlier you make your contribution, the longer your money will grow tax-deferred. Make your contribution as early as you can.

Not only do you get a tax deduction, you also receive the benefit of tax-deferred compounding when you invest in an RRSP. This is also known as sheltering your investments from income taxes. Check it out.

cheque to your RRSP. You can set up an automatic monthly mutual fund purchase plan where the money will automatically come out of your bank account and go right into your RRSP into the mutual fund you have pre-selected. This way you are investing earlier (before the March 1 deadline!) and the money is going to work for you sooner. On top of that, with the monthly contributions you will be taking advantage of something you have already learned—dollar cost averaging. The earlier you get the money in the RRSP the better. The bottom line—maximize your yearly RRSP contributions.

Types of Retirement Savings Plans and Other Assorted Perks

Basically, there are two types of RRSPs: the single-vendor RRSP (or what I call the conventional RRSP) and the self-directed RRSP. Single vendor, or conventional RRSPs, invest in one or more of a variety of mutual funds, which are held in trust under the plan by a particular issuer, bank, or trust company. There is a usually a trustee fee charged for this type of plan.

A self-directed retirement savings plan or SDRSP is slightly different from the conventional RRSP. As the name implies, it is fully self-directed. This type of plan offers you maximum flexibility in meeting your financial planning objectives and taking advantage of investment opportunities. Along with savings options, you can also invest in stocks, bonds, T-bills, GICs, RRSP-eligible mutual funds, foreign investments, and even your own mortgage.

An SDRSP can be set up at any brokerage firm and carries an annual administration fee of approximately $100 to $125. However, the fee may be substantially less if you are investing only in mutual funds. The key feature of the SDRSP is that it allows you to consolidate all your RRSP holdings into one account. So instead of receiving several statements in the mail each month (e.g., bank RRSP statement, mutual fund RRSP statement, brokerage firm RRSP statement), you'll receive just one. Having a SDRSP will not only cut down on administration fees, but also enable you to manage your money more effectively. As well, because SDRSPs are offered mainly by brokerage firms, you will have the professional services of a broker overseeing your account.

If you are just starting out, you can set up a single vendor or conventional RRSP at your local bank or mutual fund company. These RRSPs are qualified RRSPs, meaning they are limited to certain investments and don't cover the broad range of products that the SDRSPs do. If you open an RRSP account at the bank, the bank usually charges no administration fees, but you will have access to a limited range of securities and/or mutual funds. Mutual fund companies will charge you administration fees, but you have access only to that particular company's mutual funds. So, as your account grows and you contribute more into your RRSP during your peak earning years, you may find the need to switch over to an SDRSP. It is never too early to set up an SDRSP, and if the value of your RSP is approaching $10,000 to $15,000, you should certainly consider one.

The Key Advantages of an SDRSP

An SDRSP has many advantages:

➤ You control every aspect of your retirement savings program (that's where the self-directed part comes in).

➤ You have access to the widest range of investment products (different mutual fund families, stocks, bonds, T-bills, GICs, and foreign investments).

➤ You enjoy convenience: all your RRSP investments are consolidated in one place, with one statement, for easy record-keeping.

➤ You can rely on service and sound advice from the broker overseeing the SDRSP.

Spousal RRSPs

You can make tax-deductible contributions to your spouse's RRSP through a spousal RRSP. The total of both contributions (your own and your contribution to your spouse's RRSP) cannot exceed your RRSP contribution limit. You can use spousal RRSPs as an income-splitting vehicle that will allow you to pay less tax on the withdrawals from your RRSP. The advantage at retirement will be that you and your spouse will each have taxable income. The marginal tax rate on the two smaller incomes will be lower than the rate on one large income. So, if you are making the contribution, you get the tax deduction on your return, but the money can be invested in your spouse's name.

For example, Joe Smith's contribution limit is $10,000 and he contributes the ten grand to his wife's SDRSP, which is set up as spousal account (to set up an account as spousal, simply contact your broker). Joe will get the tax savings and his wife will have the $10,000 invested in her name in her SDRSP. When the RRSP matures, the money withdrawn will be taxed at his wife's lower rate, assuming she has less taxable income than Joe. Keep in mind that if that $10,000 is withdrawn from Joe's wife's account within two years of the contribution, it will be taxed at Joe's marginal tax rate. Using this strategy, husbands and wives can mature their plans separately, pay tax on the funds separately, and, ultimately, reduce their income taxes.

Technobabble

Spousal RRSPs allow couples to split their income, so that they collectively will pay less income tax.

Group RRSPs

If your company has a group RRSP, you can automatically contribute a substantial percent of your pretax dollars. The rule of thumb is to contribute the maximum amount allowable. Companies sometimes match your contribution, which allows you to save even more. The contributed monies are invested in various types of mutual funds and stock, depending on what the company offers. Remember, the advantage of any RRSP is that you can shelter all the money that is invested in the plan from taxes until you retire. At that point, you'll probably be in a lower tax bracket. You also benefit from the tax-free returns you have earned along the way. This is known as compounding and is an extremely powerful part of investing, especially in a tax-sheltered account.

Attention, First-Time Home Buyers

An SDRSP offers you investment products you would otherwise not have access to. One unique opportunity is The First-Time Home Buyers Plan. This plan allows you to take up to $20,000 cash from your RRSP to use as a down payment toward your first home, if you qualify for the program. Some of the requirements include: the house that is being purchased is your first and that the funds have been in your RRSP for at least ninety days. The money being used from your RSP must be paid back to your RSP within fifteen years. Each year you are required to pay back a minimum of one-fifteenth of the amount owed. Failure to do so will result in one-fifteenth of the amount borrowed being taxed at your marginal tax rate. In other words, you will be taxed on that amount. Consult your broker for complete details on the program.

Sidelines

Buying your first home? Check out The First-Time Home Buyers Plan. This Plan allows you to take up to $20,000 cash out of your RRSP to use as a down payment toward your first home.

I Can Hold a What in my RRSP?

Now that you have your first home, what about the mortgage? Guess what? You can even hold a mortgage in your SDRSP. If you are in a position to take a mortgage loan from a financial institution, then you are a candidate to hold that mortgage in your SDRSP. First, you must have the capital to cover the entire mortgage amount in your SDRSP. Also, the property that the mortgage covers has to meet a few requirements. For example, it has to be a Canadian residential property or a rental property that is six units or less and the mortgage in question must be a first or second mortgage. (Consult your bank representative or broker for details.) Basically, the process is the same as applying for a mortgage from a financial institution but, instead of the money coming from the financial institution, the money comes from your SDRSP.

Keep in mind that the terms of the mortgage in your SDRSP have to be within those of a normal mortgage, i.e., the interest charged has to be within the context of the market. Once the mortgage is set up in your account, your SDRSP will earn a rate equivalent to the interest on the mortgage. In other words, the money used for the mortgage

Sidelines

You've Reached Your Retirement—Now What?

It is never to early to start your RRSP but it can be too late. RRSPs have a limited life. You can maintain your RRSP until the end of the year in which you turn 69. At that time, or anytime before that, you must convert your accumulated RRSP savings using one of the following avenues:

• Withdraw all funds and pay tax on the full amount in the year of the withdrawal.

• Purchase an annuity.

• Establish a Registered Retirement Income Fund (RRIF).

When you convert your RSP to an annuity or a RRIF you will be required to withdraw a certain amount each year. (See Table 19.1)

will grow inside your SDRSP at the rate that the mortgage is set at. Consult your broker to see if it makes sense for you to set a mortgage up in your SDRSP. Some annual fees may apply. Keep in mind that if you set up a mortgage in your SDRSP, it would be the same as purchasing a bond. Think of the mortgage as a type of fixed-income product.

Table 19.1 Selected Ages and Minimum Prescribed RRIF Withdrawals

Age at end of year	% that must be withdrawn from RRIF
69	4.76
75	7.85
80	8.75
85	10.33
90	13.62
94+	20.00

Note: The above withdrawal percentages apply to RRIFs opened in or after 1993 and may change in future years.

To calculate the required Annual Minimum Payment (AMP), you multiply the value of your RRIF plan at the beginning of the year by the appropriate percentage, according to your age.

Your Registered Retirement Income Fund

When you collapse your RRSP at age 69, don't take the money and run. Although the thought is appealing, it will result in a huge tax bill as the entire amount of the withdrawal is taxable.

You do have other options. Your best option probably would be to establish a Registered Retirement Income Fund (RRIF). If you convert to a RRIF, (yes you can convert to a self-directed RRIF), you will maintain the flexibility that you had over your investments in your SDRSP. The major difference will be that you are not able to contribute into the plan anymore and that you are required to take a certain amount out each year (as described above). Or you could purchase an annuity, which is like purchasing a bond. It has a certain term to maturity and a certain interest rate. The annuity will simply pay out the prescribed amount each year.

With a SDRIF you will have the ability to take out more than the minimum prescribed withdrawals as well as control your assets in the account. If you do select the SDRIF route, remember that it is your responsibility to make sure there is enough cash in the account (you may have to sell a stock or maybe purchase a bond with large enough interest payments) to meet the amount that will be withdrawn to meet the government's requirements.

> **Sidelines**
>
> A self-directed RRIF gives you the same flexibility as a SDRSP, but the main difference is that you cannot make any contributions to the plan.

And for the Kids...

Investing for your child's post-secondary education can start as early as the day the little critter is born. If you're thinking along these lines, consider implementing a Registered Education Savings Plan (RESP).

Bet You Didn't Know

The average cost of tuition, room, and board for university has skyrocketed... and the increases won't cease. Experts now project that, assuming a modest 3 percent inflation rate over the next fifteen years, a four-year program could run you from $31,000 to $44,000 per child! An RESP is a unique opportunity to set aside money for the post-secondary education of a child or beneficiary. The money invested is allowed to grow and compound, sheltered from tax. With an RESP, you contribute up to $4000 a year to a trust that is set up in the name of a specific child or a number of beneficiaries. Each child's transactions should be recorded to protect the money set aside in that child's name. Although your contribution is not tax-deductible, investment income and capital gains that are earned and accumulated are not taxed while they remain within the RESP. When the money is used to pay the costs of a qualifying post-secondary education, the student pays tax only on the earnings portion of the withdrawal. The principal portion is not taxed. Since a student's income tends to be low, it is likely that the tax on withdrawals will be minimal or may not even apply.

Even better, the recently introduced Canada Education Savings Grant gives you an additional 20 percent on the first $2000 in annual contributions for children up to the age of 18. The maximum annual grant is $400 per child. If you can't take advantage of the full grant offered, you can carry forward this amount to future years.

To put this in perspective, let's say you decide to open an RESP at a brokerage firm. You invest $50 a month for the next twenty years with an 8 percent annual return and you will have almost $30,000.

How an RESP Works

As the planholder (known as the subscriber), you can make annual contributions of up to $4,000 into each Plan. Your lifetime limit for each RESP is $42,000. After 21 years, no further contributions are permitted to each Plan. (By the way, if you did make the maximum $4,000 contribution per year for the next 21 years at an annual return of 8 percent—you'd have more than $90,000.) The Plan must be collapsed (and all funds withdrawn) by the end of the 25th year following the year in which the plan was set up.

You are allowed to set up as many RESPs as you wish. However, no subscriber can make a person a beneficiary of more than one RESP and any beneficiary may have only one RESP. You can choose either a single beneficiary or multiple beneficiaries for your plan. However, in a multiple beneficiary plan, the beneficiaries must be related to you, either by blood or adoption.

In order to receive funds from the RESP, your beneficiary must be a student at a qualifying post-secondary educational institution and enrolled in a qualifying education program. For tax purposes, the beneficiary must include a portion of educational assistance payments into income. While the subscriber of a Plan cannot change, the beneficiaries of the Plan can be changed by the subscriber. As the subscriber, you can have your original contributions to the Plan refunded at any time, tax-free (because the money was taxed before contribution). The interest, dividends, and capital gains can continue to grow sheltered from taxes until the Plan is collapsed. In the past, income earned in the plan was lost if the beneficiary did not attend a qualifying post-secondary institution within the prescribed time limits. Recent changes allow this income to be withdrawn by the subscriber on a taxable basis provided that the plan is at least ten years old. These funds are subject to an additional 20 percent tax if the funds are withdrawn because the beneficiary did not attend a qualifying institution. In order to avoid this additional tax, the contributor may choose to transfer the contents of the RESP to his or her RRSP up to the available contribution room.

Technobabble

You can make annual contributions up to $4000 into an RESP, up to a lifetime limit of $42,000.

The Least You Need to Know

➤ Remember the golden rule of retirement planning: invest early, invest often! You want time on your side and the power of compounding working for you.

➤ Take full advantage of the tax-sheltered plans the government offers. These include RRSPs, RRIFs, and RESPs.

➤ The legislated RRSP contribution limit equals the previous year's unused contribution room plus 18 percent of last year's earned income to a maximum of $13,500.

➤ Remember to maximize your yearly RRSP contributions!

➤ Don't overlook some of the unique opportunities RRSPs offer, including the Self-directed RRSP, Spousal RRSPs, The First-Time Home Buyers Plan, and Mortgages.

Mutual Funds and Taxes

You're off and running with your new mutual fund investments—headfirst, you hope, into a bull market. Everything is going great. That is, until you're faced with the sudden realization that it's time to deal with Revenue Canada. Ugh!

You've now come upon one of the sad truths about mutual fund investing. Unfortunately, we all must pay taxes on our mutual fund earnings. At the beginning of each new year, you're reminded of this fact when you get the tax statements from your mutual fund company.

This chapter examines your mutual fund taxes and suggests ways to reduce the tax bite. You'll learn how different types of income are taxed and how to make the best use of any losses you may incur.

Yikes! Taxman's Gonna Get Ya!

There's no getting around it, people. Unless you are investing in a tax-sheltered account, once you start making some bucks in your mutual fund, Revenue Canada wants a piece of it.

When you invest money outside a tax-sheltered account, you pay taxes on three different sources of income from your mutual funds—capital gains income, dividend income, and interest income. At the beginning of each calendar year, the mutual fund company will send you a T-3 slip, which breaks down each of the three types of income earned in the previous year. Each is taxed differently.

➤ **Interest Income**: This is income from any fixed-income investments such as bonds and money market securities. Interest income is taxed at your full marginal tax rate.

➤ **Dividend distributions**. This is income from stock dividends that the fund's portfolio has earned during the taxable year. Dividends are taxed more favourably than regular income (e.g., interest income). You are entitled to a dividend gross-up and credit from dividends you receive from taxable Canadian corporations. For example, if you receive $1000 in dividends, you would be entitled to a 25 percent gross-up, which equals $1250. The $1250 is subject to federal tax. But— you can then claim a federal tax credit of 13.33 percent. Provincial tax is then deducted. The exact calculation looks like this:

Canadian Dividend Gross-Up and Credit Calculation

Dividend Income:	$1,000
Gross-Up (25% of $1000)	250
Taxable Income	$1,250
Federal Tax (e.g., 26% of $1250)	325
Federal Tax Credit (13.33% of $1250)	167
Federal Tax Payable ($325 – $167)	158
Provincial Tax	84
(e.g., 53% of $158 (federal tax payable)	
Total taxes payable ($158 + $84)	242
Net Dividend	$758

➤ **Capital gains distributions**. This is the net profit that the fund earns from the sale of the mutual fund portfolio holdings. When a fund sells securities that have risen in value, it takes a profit. Any losses from the sale of securities that have declined in value are subtracted from the profits, however. Capital gains are taxed at your full marginal tax rate, but only taxed on three-quarters of the capital gain amount.

Depending on the type of mutual fund you have invested in, it is possible not to have any reported interest, dividends, or capital gains for a particular year. However, if you do not receive any tax slips in the new year, be sure to call your advisor or mutual fund company representative to confirm.

Revenue Canada Takes Its Cut

You have to pay tax on any fund units sold at a profit. If you sell a portion of your mutual fund holdings for a profit, you have to pay tax on that profit, which is called a capital gain. How that profit is calculated can get a little bit complicated. If you owned the fund for a long time, chances are you have received distributions of dividends, interest, or capital gains that have probably been reinvested back into the fund. On top of that, you may or may not have put some new money into the fund. In calculating your capital gain, you already know the sale price, but what about calculating the cost price? Listed below are a couple of ways in which to calculate your gain.

First In, First Out (FIFO). With this method, as you sell units of a fund, you assume that the units you are selling are the first ones you bought. Their cost basis, therefore, is the cost related to the oldest units of the fund in your portfolio. Here's an example. Let's assume you hold the following 300 units of a fund: 100 that you bought in January 1993 at $10 a unit, 100

Hot Tip

Many investors overpay their tax on capital gains or profits because they fail to figure accurately the average cost of their units. Take the time to add up all the units you bought.

Hot Tip

It's advisable to consult with your accountant or tax attorney before you decide on a method for paying taxes on the sale of your mutual fund units.

that you bought directly or through reinvestment of distributions in January 1994 at $11 a unit, and 100 units that you bought in January 1995 at $12 a unit. Under FIFO, when you go to sell 100 units, you assume those 100 are the ones you bought first in January 1993 at $10 a unit.

Drawback: With this method, you can pay whopping capital gains taxes when you sell fund units you've owned for a long time. Of course, if your fund's net asset value has declined, this is not the case.

Last In, First Out (LIFO). With this method, as you sell units of a fund, you assume that the units you are selling are the last ones you bought. Their cost basis, therefore, is the cost related to the newest units of the fund in your portfolio. So, going back to our original FIFO example, you would use the shares bought in January 1995 at $12 as the ones you sold.

Technobabble

A *loss carry forward* is when a mutual fund with losses in one year opts to carry those losses over to a future year, providing investors with a potential tax break in a subsequent year.

Sidelines

Capital losses can be carried backward three years to be applied against capital gains, or can be carried forward indefinitely to be used against any future capital gains.

Drawback: With this method, you may end up with a capital loss, as you may not have held the fund long enough to generate a profit. If you anticipate a capital loss, make sure you have capital gains to offset them because you can reduce the amount of capital gains tax you pay. For example, if you have $1000 worth of gains in one tax year and $1000 worth of losses, you can net the losses against the gains and not have any taxable income from your investments.

Average Price Per Share. With this method—the most popular—you figure your profits by first factoring the total cost of all the fund units you bought and dividing that by the number of units you bought. This gives you the average cost you paid for all your units. Suppose you paid $8000 for all your units and now have 400 units of the fund. The average cost is $20 a unit. If you sold all 400 units at $22 per unit, your capital gain for tax purposes is a $2 per-unit gain multiplied by 400 units. This equals $800. If you sold just 100 units, you take the same $2 gain and multiply it by 100.

Drawback: This is the middle-of-the-road method of figuring taxes due on the sale of fund units. Unless the value of your units has decreased, you pay less in taxes than you do under the FIFO method. However, you might pay more to Revenue Canada than if you had sold specified units. What do you do if you've been socking away $50 to $100 a month into a mutual fund for years via an automatic investment plan? How do you figure the cost of all those units? Fortunately, many mutual fund groups send you a year-end report that lists the average cost of all the units you've directly purchased or obtained from reinvestment of distributions. Then you or your accountant can figure any net capital gains based on the sale price of all the fund's units.

If you don't get a report, you have to go back and calculate the average cost of the fund's units yourself. Be sure to keep all your mutual fund confirmation statements through the years. Most funds have records going back at least 10 years, in case you are missing some statements.

Six Tips On Mutual Fund Taxes

As the Scout's motto indicates, it's always best to "be prepared." Here are several ways to make paying taxes on your mutual funds a less frustrating affair:

Not all fund distributions are alike. Make sure that you report dividends from the fund as dividends on your tax return. By contrast, capital gains distributions and interest are reported on different lines. As all three types of income are taxed differently, they must be separated on your return.

Wait until after the fund's ex-dividend date to buy fund units. The ex-dividend date is the date on which the value of the income or capital gains distribution is deducted from the net asset value (NAV) of the fund's units. The distribution deducted from the NAV of a fund you just bought is returned to you or reinvested in new units. However, you'll end up paying taxes on this distribution. That's right—you'll pay taxes on money that you just paid out as part of the purchase price of the units!

Keep good records of all your mutual fund transactions. File all your confirmation statements as well as your monthly or quarterly statements. You'll need the information when you file your income taxes.

Watch out for distributions from your fund. The T-3 form shows the breakdown of distributions between dividends, interest, and capital gains.

Remember that capital gains and dividends are taxed more favourably than interest income.

Managing Your Estate

Estate planning is beyond the scope of this book but it is something that you should address with your investment advisor, financial planner, or accountant. The first thing to do when estate planning is to draw up a will. If you already have a will, review it and update it if necessary. There are ways to minimize estate taxes so that your loved ones may gain the maximum benefit of your estate. Consultation with an advisor is recommended here.

Technobabble

A fund's *ex-dividend date* is the date on which the value of the income or capital gains distribution is deducted from the price of a fund's units. Buying a fund just prior to that date could result in an investor paying taxes for the year on units that were just bought.

Hot Tip

You can avoid all the tax hassles that Revenue Canada imposes by keeping your money in tax-sheltered plans. Your money grows tax-deferred in RRSPs, RESPs, and RRIFs. You needn't worry about paying taxes on fund dividends and capital gains distributions or capital gains on the sale of fund units until you withdraw the funds.

The Least You Need to Know

➤ You must pay taxes on mutual fund distributions.

➤ You must pay taxes on profitable sales of mutual fund units.

➤ The investment company sends you forms (T-3s) stating the amount you must declare as taxable income.

➤ The average price per share method is the most frequently used method to calculate taxes on the sale of mutual fund units.

➤ Take advantage of tax strategies you can use to cut your tax bite.

Glossary

Aggressive growth funds Mutual funds that strive for maximum growth (increases in the unit price) as the primary objective. Also known as small company or small-cap funds.

Annual report This is a financial statement issued by a company that shows all of its pluses and minuses, including whether the company made a profit or not.

Annual return The percentage of change in a mutual fund's net asset value over a year's time, factoring in income dividend payments, capital gains, and reinvestment of these distributions.

Asset-allocation fund Balanced fund in which changes are made in the stock and bond percentage mix, based on the outlook for each market.

Automatic investment plan Program that allows you to have as little as $25 a month electronically deducted from your chequing account and invested in the mutual fund of your choice.

Average price per share Most popular method of paying taxes on mutual fund sales, in which you calculate gains or losses by first figuring an average cost per unit. You calculate the total cost of all the fund units you own and divide that by the number of units you own.

Balanced funds Mutual funds that invest in both stocks and bonds.

Bankers Acceptance (BA) Short-term loan to companies that export worldwide. It is secured by goods that are to be sold.

Bear market Period during which the stock market typically loses more than 10 percent of its value.

Blue-chip stocks Stocks issued by well-established companies that pay dividends.

Bond A debt instrument issued by a company, city, or province, or the Canadian government or its agencies, with a promise to pay regular interest and return the principal on a specified date.

Bull market Period during which the stock market typically moves higher for a couple of years straight.

Canadian Treasury bond funds Mutual funds that invest in Canadian Treasury bonds and notes.

Canadian Treasury bonds Debt instruments directly backed by the Canadian Treasury.

Canadian securities Generally, Treasury notes, bills, or bonds issued and guaranteed by the Canadian government.

Capital gains Profits on the sale of securities.

Closed-end funds Funds whose units are traded on an exchange, similar to stocks. The price per unit doesn't typically equal the net asset value of a unit. Mutual funds are not closed-end funds.

Commercial paper Short-term loans to corporations.

Common stock Unit of ownership in a public corporation with voting rights, but with lower priority than either preferred stock or bonds if the company is ever liquidated.

Convertible bond funds Mutual funds that invest in bonds that can be converted into stocks.

Corporate bonds Debt instruments issued by corporations.

Custodian Bank or other financial institution that safeguards mutual fund securities and may respond to transactions only by designated fund officers.

Distributions Dividends income and capital gains generally paid by mutual fund companies to their shareholders.

Diversification Investing in a variety of investments to lessen risk.

Diversified Spread out, as among a variety of investments that perform differently.

Dividends Profits that a corporation or mutual fund distributes to shareholders.

Dollar cost averaging Strategy of making regular investments into a mutual fund and having earnings automatically reinvested. This way, when the unit price drops, more units are bought at lower prices.

Dow Jones Industrial Average Model for the overall stock market that tracks the performance of 30 U.S. blue-chip stocks.

Equities Stock, or ownership of shares in a company.

Ex-dividend date Date on which the value of the income or capital gains distribution is deducted from the price of a fund's units.

Face value Value of a bond or note as given on the certificate. Corporate bonds are usually issued with $1000 face values, municipal bonds with $5000 face values, and government bonds, $1000 to $10,000 face values. Also known as the principal.

First In-First Out (FIFO) Basis for calculating the tax impact of mutual fund profits and losses that assumes shares sold are the oldest shares owned.

Fixed-income fund Another term for a mutual bond fund.

Front-end loads Sales commission paid upfront when you purchase a mutual fund.

Global funds Mutual funds that invest in both Canada and foreign countries. Also known as world funds.

Growth funds Mutual funds that usually invest in the non-dividend-paying common stock of mid- and larger-sized companies with expansion potential. Growth funds provide capital gains potential rather than income.

Guaranteed Investment Certificates (GICs) Debt instruments issued by banks requiring a minimum investment at a predetermined rate of interest for a stated term. These are generally non-redeemable and non-transferable prior to maturity.

Hedging Strategy of investing in one or more securities to protect yourself from potential losses in other investments.

High-yield bond funds Riskier bond mutual funds that invest in high-yield bonds of companies with lower credit ratings.

Income Periodic interest or dividend distributions obtained from a fund.

Inflation Rise in prices of goods and services.

Inflation hedge Term describing an investment that performs well when inflation heats up.

Interest income Earnings received, often from bonds.

International bonds Debt instruments issued by foreign governments or corporations.

International funds Mutual funds that invest in stocks or bonds of worldwide companies.

Investment banker Firm that sells stocks or bonds to brokerages that, in turn, sell them to investors on a securities exchange.

Investment company Firm that, for a management fee, invests pooled funds of small investors in securities appropriate for its stated investment objectives.

Investment advisor Individual who provides investment advice to clients and executes trades on their behalf in securities and other investment products.

Investment objective Description, included in a fund prospectus, of what a mutual fund hopes to accomplish.

Last In, First Out (LIFO) Basis for calculating the tax impact of mutual fund profits and losses that assumes units sold are those most recently purchased.

Management fee Charge for running the fund.

Market timing Strategy by which investors attempt to buy low and sell high by buying when the market is turning bearish and selling at the end of a bull market.

Maturity date Date that a bond is due for payoff.

Money market mutual fund Mutual fund that invests typically in short-term government and company loans and BAs. These funds tend to be lower-yielding, but less risky than most other types of funds. Also known as money market funds.

Mortgage-Backed Security (MBS) Similar to bonds, MBSs are backed by a share in a pool of home mortgages under the *National Housing Act*. You receive monthly payments or interest and principal re-payments.

Net asset value Per-share value of your fund's investments. Also known as share price or net asset value per share (NAVPS).

No-load mutual fund Mutual fund that is sold without sales commission.

Note Another word for short-term bond.

Open-end funds Funds that permit ongoing purchase and redemption of fund units (mutual funds are open-end funds).

Over-the-counter market Market that uses a network of brokers to buy and sell securities rather than an exchange.

Portfolio manager Person responsible for making mutual fund investments.

Precious metals mutual fund Mutual funds that invest in precious metals and mining stocks.

Preferred stock Type of stock that takes priority over common stock in the payment of dividends or if the company is liquidated.

Principal Original investment.

Prospectus Legal disclosure document that spells out information you need to know to make an investment decision on a mutual fund or other security.

Rebalancing Investment strategy in which you adjust your mix of investments periodically to keep the proper percentages of money in each fund, based on your tolerance for risk.

Regional funds Mutual funds that invest in one specific region of the globe.

Registered representative Person licensed to sell stocks, bonds, mutual funds, and other types of securities.

Registered Retirement Savings Plan (RRSP) A vehicle available to individuals to defer tax on specified amounts of money to be used for retirement. The holder invests the money in one or more of a variety of investments that are held in trust under the plan. Income tax on the contributions and earnings within the plan are deferred until the money is withdrawn at retirement. RRSPs can be transferred into Registered Retirement Income Funds upon investor's retirement.

Registered Retirement Income Fund (RRIF) A tax-deferred vehicle available to RRSP holders. The plan holder invests the funds in the RRIF upon retirement and must withdraw a certain amount each year. Income tax is payable on the withdrawal amounts.

Repurchase agreements Generally, overnight loans secured by Canadian Treasury securities.

Risk Chance of losing money.

Risk tolerance Amount of money you can stomach losing in a given year.

S&P 500 index Measure of the performance of a large group of blue-chip stocks in the United States.

Secondary market Market wherein bonds, stocks, or other securities are bought and sold after they're already issued.

Securities Stocks, bonds, or rights to ownership, such as options, typically sold by a broker.

Securities exchange Tightly regulated marketplace where stocks, bonds, and cash are traded.

Share Unit of ownership.

Shareholder One who owns shares. In a mutual fund, this person has voting rights.

Single-country funds Mutual funds or closed-end funds that invest in one country.

Socially responsible funds Mutual funds that invest in companies that don't pollute the environment or sell arms. These funds will not own tobacco or alcohol stocks, nor invest in companies with poor employee relations.

Specialty funds Funds that invest in one specific industry or industry sector.

Speculation Gambling on a risky investment in hopes of a high payoff down the road.

Stock Investment that buys ownership in a corporation in exchange for a portion of that company's earnings and assets.

Stockbroker Person licensed to sell stocks and other types of securities.

Total return The rate of return on an investment, including reinvestment of distributions.

Treasury bills Short-term IOUs to the Canadian Treasury.

TSE 300 The Toronto Stock Exchange 300 Index, which tracks 300 of the most widely traded stocks in Canada.

World funds Mutual funds that invest in both Canada and foreign countries. Also known as global funds.

Yield Interest or market earnings on a bond or other investment.

Mutual Funds: Information and Education

IFIC (The Investment Funds Institute of Canada)

IFIC is a national trade association for the mutual fund industry. IFIC provides both general information to the public as well as educational courses and licensing to members of the industry. You can reach them at the following address:

The Investment Funds Institute of Canada
151 Yonge St.
5th Floor
Toronto, ON
M5C 2W7
Tel: (416) 363-2158
Web site: www.ific.ca

Top-Ten Mutual Fund Companies by Assets Under Administration

(From largest to smallest, as at June 1998 according to the Investment Funds Institute of Canada)

Please note that all of the following mutual fund companies have offices across Canada. You can reach your nearest office by calling the toll-free numbers as listed. (Some numbers may not be accessible across Canada.)

Investors Group
(888) 746-6344

Royal Mutual Funds Inc.
(800) 463-3863

Trimark Investment Management Inc.
(800) 465-3399

Mackenzie Financial Corporation
(888) 653-7070

Templeton Management Limited
(800) 387-0830

Fidelity Investments Canada Limited
(888) 203-4778

AGF Management Limited
(800) 268-8583

TD Asset Management Inc.
(800) 268-8166

CIBC Securities Inc.
(800) 465-3863

CT (Canada Trust) Investment Management Group
(800) 386-3757

Index

More Great Canadian Complete Idiot's Guides!

If you liked this *Complete Idiot's Guide,* check out these other titles!

The Complete Idiot's Guide to Managing Your Money in Canada

by Robert K. Heady, Christy Heady, and Bruce McDougall

The key to financial success is simple—good money management. *The Complete Idiot's Guide to Managing Your Money in Canada* gives readers the inside scoop on all the latest in financial planning plus an informative explanation of all the basics. Learn about mortgages, insurance, mutual funds, chequing and savings accounts and much, much more.

288 pages
$21.95
ISBN 0-13-080935-7

The Complete Idiot's Guide to Making Money in the Canadian Stock Market

by Christy Heady and Stephen Nelson

The Complete Idiot's Guide to Making Money in the Canadian Stock Market helps you make sense of the complicated world of finance. You will discover the best financial strategies, feel confident about investing your money and build your wealth with the help of this exciting new guide.

---

368 pages
$24.95
ISBN 0-13-779134-8

The Complete Idiot's Guide to Getting Rich in Canada

by Larry Waschka and Bruce McDougall

Many Canadians want a worry-free retirement, neat stuff, freedom of choice and security—in other words, they want to be rich! In this comprehensive new book you will learn all the essential techniques, attitudes and perspectives required to live the good life. This guide provides clear advice on the how to build your personal fortune and achieve your dreams of grandeur—with ease!

---

352 pages
$21.95
ISBN 0-13-080127-5

The Complete Idiot's Guide to Personal Finance for Canadians—New Edition

by Bruce McDougall

Packed with information on investment strategies, tax changes, stock market trends and RRSPs, plus all the essential money basics, *The Complete Idiot's Guide to Personal Finance for Canadians* is an updated version of a Canadian bestseller. This informative book is the ultimate guide for those who want to invest and save with confidence.

---

272 pages
$19.95
ISBN 0-13-080126-7